"August, authoritative compass both the life Transition.' The setting is unique, positioned to glean practical life lessons from raw temporal experience, refined by eternal wisdom, revealed in the grand narrative of scripture – the source of our world-view. Negotiating tough transitions calls for a clear understanding of both. We journeyed together for 25 rich years. I benefited vicariously from his mentorship. Together we tested ideas. Many under his care will attest to the joy of restored hope. Now – you the reader – can also share in the accumulative wisdom from the life of one who has modelled servant leadership."

—*Dr. Ken Gamble,*
President, Missionary Health Institute/International Health Management, Toronto, ON, Canada

"In his new book, *Pastors in Transition*, Glenn Taylor discusses a very important ministry issue using great ideas and solid practical research, both tested for years in the crucible of real life. As one of the hundreds of people who Glenn has assisted in a ministry transition, I can affirm personally the effectiveness of the clear principles and practical advice he shares creatively for the benefit of all."

—*Rev. Marvin Brubacher,*
Executive Director, MentorLink, Canada, former President, Heritage Bible College and Seminary, Canada

"Glenn has skillfully presented his years of experience, wisdom and research in dealing with transitions in ministry. This book is an invaluable resource for ministry families to successfully negotiate the inevitable changes that occur over the course of lives spent in ministry. I enthusiastically recommend it to all pastors, missionaries and their wives."

—*Kim Lidstone*,
Member Care & Candidate Coordinator,
Fellowship International, FEBC, Canada

"A must read book for anyone that is in a transitioning stage of their lives. Every church board should have one in their library to help prepare them for exiting or entering pastors. In keeping with Glenn's metaphors of camping, canoeing and crossing rivers, this book is the "Swiss army knife" of resources."

—*Rev. Reid Cooke*,
Retired Pastor, Associate Gospel Churches, Chaplain:
Christian Legal Fellowship, Canada

"This book is to a pastor in transition what a paddle is to a canoe; it will guide you, direct you, stabilize you through the rapids, and provide you a prop to pause and reflect on your course."

—*David R. Johnson*,
Pastor, Minden Associate Gospel Church, Ontario

"This is a very practical summary of Glenn's lifetime of ministry of pastoring pastors, and a good read for any pastor. Whether in transition or not presently, you will at some time."

—*Dr. Rodger McCready*,
Pastor, ON, Canada

PASTORS
in
TRANSITION

PASTORS *in* TRANSITION

NAVIGATING *the* TURBULENCE *of* CHANGE

GLENN C. TAYLOR

PASTORS IN TRANSITION
Copyright © 2013 by Glenn C. Taylor

All rights reserved. Neither this publication nor any part of this publication may be reproduced or transmitted in any form or by any means, electronic or mechanical, including photocopying, recording or any information storage and retrieval system, without permission in writing from the author.

All scriptures are taken from the Holy Bible, NEW INTERNATIONAL VERSION® unless otherwise indicated. Copyright © 1973, 1978, 1984, 2011 by Biblica, Inc. All rights reserved worldwide. Used by permission.

ISBN: 978-1-77069-814-7

Printed in Canada

Word Alive Press
131 Cordite Road, Winnipeg, MB R3W 1S1
www.wordalivepress.ca

WORD ALIVE PRESS
Just Write!

MIX
Paper from
responsible sources
FSC   FSC® C016245

Library and Archives Canada Cataloguing in Publication

Taylor, Glenn (Glenn Calvin), 1935-
    Pastors in transition : navigating the turbulence of change / Glenn C. Taylor.

ISBN 978-1-77069-814-7

    1. Clergy--Relocation. 2. Clergy--Office. I. Title.

BV664.T39 2013   253   C2013-900459-9

Dedication

*To the endurance of all called
to serve in vocational ministry*

Table of Contents

PREFACE xi
ACKNOWLEDGMENTS xiii
INTRODUCTION xvii
CHAPTER 1 1
   The Challenge of Changing Ministries
CHAPTER 2 19
   Pastors in Transition
CHAPTER 3 33
   The Transition Experience
CHAPTER 4 51
   Responding to Transitions
CHAPTER 5 75
   Facing the Prospects of a New Ministry
CHAPTER 6 93
   Finding One's Place in Ministry
CHAPTER 7 111
   Perspectives on One's Role in Ministry
CHAPTER 8 131
   Meeting the Challenges of Ministry
CHAPTER 9 157
   The Care & Maintenance of Pastors
CHAPTER 10 183
   A Biblical Account of Commitment, Failure, and Restoration
CHAPTER 11 195
   Postscript: Where Do We Go from Here?
ABOUT THE AUTHOR 199

Preface

Change is a constant in life. It is sometimes sought but often feared. It excites and challenges, and it frequently shakes the foundations of our stability and comfort. The permanence and shalom that we find restful is disturbed. Change may be defined in many ways; it may be seen as disruption, permutation, modulation, transformation, fear of the unknown, exploration of what's new, or metamorphosis. It may be preceded by repentance, restlessness, excitement, anticipation, hope, or conflict. It is also inherent in our growth and development. We know it is coming but are often surprised when it is suddenly upon us.

Those committed to a life of ministry will frequently experience change in their journey of faith. When the life of faith is shone through the prism of life's journey, it displays all the colors of the spectrum, not in static fashion but like the northern lights—a constantly moving, shimmering experience. Life is rarely black and white. Its struggles can never be white washed by the Bible. The problem of evil and pain persist in the human drama. The abundant life consists not only of joy unspeakable; it also contains the pain of stress, conflict, rejection, and hurt.

The heroes of our faith were not flawless. Their lives involved difficulties inflicted by others, plus the consequences of their own moral failures. Job was tempted and tried in excess by Satan, with God's awareness. Later, he had his encounter with the Lord to refocus his perspective, and though there still remained ambiguity, faith triumphed! Abraham, the "friend of God," was commanded to offer his only son, reprieved at the last moment by the hand of a gracious Sovereign. David, the apple of God's eye, fell into the depths of moral failure but through repentance and a love for the Lord became one of our great examples of a man of deep faith. Paul overtly acknowledges the confusion of living with passions and desires that require a victory possible only in Christ.

The intention of this book is to examine one of the frequent causes of ambiguity for those called to serve in the chaos of a fallen world. The specific focus will be on the transition of those in ministry from one opportunity to another. It is a rarity for one to continue in one place of ministry over their entire career. Having walked with hundreds of persons who have transitioned from one challenging field of service to another, I have witnessed their process of change. These are hard experiences, even when they are passed through well, but can be devastating if they are complicated by failure, rejection, conflict, or the result of moral failure. The event can feel like abandonment, the absence of God, the dark night of the soul, or even a time of abuse and suffering.

There is much help available for understanding and growing through transition. This book will elucidate the experience and suggest effective ways that we can overtly, honestly, and humbly turn things into a time of growth and awareness of the presence of God. I recall the response of the nine-year-old boy when challenged with the question, "Where was God when the Twin Towers in New York were being destroyed?" His response was simply, "God was in the Towers with the people." God is not a spectator to our transitions in the journey of ministry but is there with us. May we each find his presence and celebrate his goodness in the midst.

Acknowledgments

Some of the most important contributors to my life have been individuals who have invited me to walk with them through the valleys and mountaintop experiences of their lives. These include scores of pastors and missionaries who gave me the privileged of journeying with them in their passion to serve God in many hard places. These are my heroes for they have given themselves for God's glory in the service of others.

I was honoured to have some highly gifted individuals from the fields of theology, psychology, psychiatry, and medicine who guided me in my desire to explore the relationship between theology and psychology. The most influential of these were Dr. Maurice Flint, specialist in pastoral care; Dr. Boothroyd, chief of psychiatry, Sunnybrook Hospital; Dr. Kenneth Gamble, president, Missionary Health Institute/International Health Management; Dr. Stuart Boehmer, a leader in theological education and pastoral ministry; Dr. Gerald Griffiths, visionary in international missions; and Miller Alloway, a skilled leader in industry with a passion for the Kingdom of God. The team of the MK-CART/CORE[1] research group in missions demanded academic and professional research with careful analysis. I hesitate to single out any of the team members, but Dr. John Powell and Dr. David Wickstrom were especially helpful in the research team in defining care in missions. Dr. Gamble, with whom I worked for eighteen years, taught me to see treatment from an evidenced-based approach and to passionately pursue an interdisciplinary model that addressed in a coordinated manner the com-

---

1   See note at end of Acknowledgements

plex problems of persons. His vision and passion for the care for those serving internationally inspired and facilitated my involvement with servants in many countries of the world.

Many other peers and colleagues have been an inspiration: Dr. Rod Wilson, who collaborated in counselling and writing when we were involved in theological education; Rev. Marvin Brubacher, who has been an inspiration and challenge as a colleague and mentor; Dr. Gordon Stephens, pastor and colleague who was my encourager for over fifty years along with his wife, Lois; many former students who have continued to challenge and question me over the years. Dr. David Pollock, former President of Interaction International, who cared more for missionary children than any other person I have known was a dear brother to me. One of my students from the 1970s deserves special mention: Bryan Carson, a prayer warrior, has been my best critic and editor in writing this book. He forces me to say what I mean in a coherent manner that hopefully makes sense to others. That is not always easy for someone like me who is interested more in the message communicated than the vehicle of language. This book would not have been possible without Bryan's technical and creative input. Dr. George Cannon has helped me to focus on pastoral and church issues. Dr. Rick Tobias inspired care for the needy. My pastor, Bruce Laidlaw, keeps the needs of the local church before me.

A constant in over fifty-five years of my life has been my wife, Mary. The trust, affirmation, and encouragement she has provided enabled me to venture into territory in ministry that I would not have imagined engaging in without her support. Her true and engaged partnership in this journey has contributed in ways God alone could identify. Along with her, Dawn and Tim, our adult children and their spouses, have blessed

Acknowledgments

me with comfort and encouragement that has freed me to explore the integration of disciplines that are often perceived to stand separately. Our seven grandsons and one granddaughter give me hope for the future. They are precious.

I celebrate God's grace and goodness over five decades of adventure and fulfillment in life that exceeded any dreams imagined in youth.

Note: MK-CART/CORE, which is known in the missions' community, requires some explanation. MK refers to missionary kids, those young people who are raised in other cultures where their parents are serving. CART refers to a group of twelve to fifteen representatives of a large number of international mission organizations. They defined concerns and questions of interest to their organizations, which they wished addressed by research. CORE was composed of six professionals who received their concerns, created research questions, conducted research, and reported back to the CART group, who determined the application in their respective missions. The work of MK-CART/CORE was reported in several peer-review journals and in a book referenced in footnotes in this book.

Introduction

We launched our canoes at 4:00 p.m., May 5th, from Harris Lake for a two-week wilderness trip east through Niascoot, Maple, and Wahwaskesh lakes to return west on the Magnetawan River. I was to guide twelve college students through this experience. The snow began to fall at 5:45 p.m. and we set up camp that evening, broke camp the next morning, and began the daily routine through fourteen days in every imaginable kind of weather on lakes, rivers, and rapids.

The experience of pastors transitioning from ministry to ministry may be seen in the analogy of breaking camp, setting off from one shore, crossing a turbulent river, and setting up camp on the other side. The skill and care with which one breaks camp will greatly influence casting off from shore, the stability and success of the crossing, and setting up camp in a new location. Leaving one ministry, for whatever reason, and beginning in a new opportunity can be a major challenge.

In this treatise on transition, my use of the word *ministry* is very inclusive; I refer to all who are engaged in any form of service for the Kingdom of God whether in an international or national setting. Thus, it includes those engaged in church ministry, missions, and parachurch activity. To simplify communication, I will use *ministry* or *pastor* in this broad sense. Experience has led me to conclude that the similarities are sufficient to warrant this approach. However, my focus in this book will have specific application to the pastor in the church community. There is a temporary aspect to ministry much like setting up camp for a period of time with the awareness that one will later move on. I am reminded of John's words concerning Jesus: "He came to that which was his own, but his own did not receive him."[2] The ministry of Jesus in his incarnation was brief. The image in this verse is that of Jesus *tenting* among humans for only a few years. Pastoral ministry has this transitory aspect to it. The imagery of a campsite from which we will soon move describes this well. A pastor is one with the humanity among whom he ministers, in contrast to Christ who was God among us. Paradoxically, he is a gift of Christ to the church, and while in their presence is to *flesh out* the ministry to which he has been called.

Also, it is important to remember that ministry involves the work of eternity. This breadth of perspective frees us from micro-focus on our brief participation in the eternal work of Christ. Paul provides a healthy perspective of the eternal supremacy of Christ. "For by him all things were created: things in heaven and earth, visible and invisible…He is before all things, and in him all things hold together. And he is the head of the body, the church."[3] This view engenders a humility that frees us from a perspective that is too personal and self-focused.

Very few pastors stay in one camp for the life of their ministry. Most in our culture move on average every four years. Thus, there are many transitions along one's career path. The first chapter of this book will illustrate the challenges of transition and introduce a process by which to reflect upon it. In chapter two, transition will be defined in terms of its component parts. Understanding is a prerequisite to preparation and effective response.

That first snowstorm on our canoe trip was a shock to many. Most had not taken seriously earlier instruction about

---

2   John 1:11
3   Colossian 1:15-20

preparing and packing for an early spring canoe trip. Anticipating the adventure had dulled the openness to careful preparation. In like manner, the excitement of ministry does not prepare one for the termination of a ministry. We generally do not enter an opportunity with a clear exit strategy! Transition out of a ministry brings surprises.

Chapter three will examine in detail the starting place (the camp) and the leaving (packing and debarking) and will introduce the heart of transition. We define this as *The In-Between* stage of transition. It is often like traversing a tumultuous river. Chapter four will discuss the various traumas related to moving through the no-man's land between ministries. In chapter five, the prospect of beginning again in a new ministry is viewed as both a challenge and an opportunity. The challenge is to deal with the residual impact of the past on oneself and one's family and to prepare to begin anew with a clear vision as to the call of God. The subsequent three chapters look at avenues to explore in a personal way one's gifts, abilities, and skills so as to help us respond to the challenge of new opportunities.

In chapter nine, the need for care and maintenance for those engaged in ministry is illustrated by the many dimensions of care accessible to pastors. It is my observation that we often put more effort into caring for our material possessions than we do in providing for our own nurture and healthy development or our relational experiences.

The tenth chapter turns to a biblical illustration from the narrative of the disciples of the Lord. The trauma they encountered between the arrest of Jesus and his ascension is instructive in regard to the losses and pain associated with transitions. Their bewilderment parallels that of people in ministry as they move through the loss or change from one ministry to another. The postscript will offer suggestions concerning our response and involvement as a consequence of our consideration of transition.

At the end of each chapter I have included some "Questions for Reflection." These are intended to evoke further thought and processing.

You will appreciate the honour given to me by many in ministry who gave me the privilege of journeying alongside them through some of the hard experiences of ministry. In our explorations, they have discovered the presence of God, the healing that comes through the ministry of the Holy Spirit, and the joy that lifts our hearts in praise through God's healing and faithfulness to his servants. My prayer is that you too will find "the God and Father of our Lord Jesus Christ, the Father of all compassion and the God of all comfort" coming alongside of you in every challenge of transition. (2 Corinthians 1:3-4)

Chapter One

The Challenge of Changing Ministries

> Don't be afraid, I've redeemed you.
> I've called your name. You're mine.
> When you're in over your head, I'll be there with you.
> When you're in rough waters, you will not go down.
> When you're between a rock and a hard place,
> it won't be a dead end –
> Because I am God, your personal God.
>
> Isaiah 43:1-3 (MSG)

The pastoral life is all about coming and going, or if you wish, coming and leaving. Leaving one church and arriving at another happens frequently for pastors. We were thirty pastors sitting around in a coffee house environment when the question was raised: "How many of the group had ministered in more than one church?" All but one had moved to new ministry opportunities. The challenge of changing ministries is a predictable constant! It happens several times along the career path for most. Having walked this path with hundreds of people in ministry, I want to share with you what this has meant for many. You will find your story reflected in the lives that are the basis for this book. How many times have you changed churches or places of ministry? Or, if you are starting out in ministry, how many times do you anticipate changing ministry over your career path?

Transitioning from one church to another is like crossing a river from one shore to the other. The river may be turbulent with rapids and whirlpools or it may be calm and peaceful. Sometimes it is wide and requires labour to debark on the other side. For some the river is narrow in that another ministry opportunity has been arranged before leaving the last one. Whether large or small, the river of transition must be crossed.

The nature of the river-crossing will be determined by many contributing factors. Many of these are determined by the cause and nature of the leaving. The crossing will be calm, turbulent, or dangerous depending on the means of conveyance and the resources used. In my travels, rivers have been crossed by several types of ferries but also by more primitive means such as cables, canoes, and rowboats. If the means was under the control of captains, they sometimes didn't function on my time line, or with efficiency. Being an outdoor enthusiast has given me many opportunities to traverse rivers by canoe, and this personal craft offers its challenges.

Transition from one side of a river to another may be as challenging as transitioning from one church to another. Most pastors will make transitions several times along their career path. They leave one shore, one place of ministry, to set up camp on another shore, another place of ministry. In crossing the river we need guidance from the God "who carves a path through the pounding waves."[4] As we will see, much depends upon the reason for leaving and the process by which we break camp. Breaking camp and traversing the river will significantly determine the experience of setting up camp in a new location.

We must explore the residual impact of the previous ministry that a pastor will carry forward, the process of transition,

---

4   Isaiah 43:16

and entrance into the new ministry. These are best carefully explored within helpful structures and processes that identify the experience of leaving, including the pain and grief of loss. Therefore, the time between ministries requires some understanding and the projection of entering a new ministry will be discussed in detail.

The term *ministry* in this book will include all the different types of vocational Christian ministry, whether in church, charitable organization, or international ministry. The term *pastor* will be used to refer to anyone involved in ministry as a career. Some choose to limit the use of the term *pastor* to refer only to a male in the top leadership role within a church. My expanded use of the term *pastor* is intended to include all individuals in ministry, whether male or female, in any setting. Those who minister in denominations with female pastors will be comfortable with the term. Women in denominations wherein the word is used in a more limited sense should feel free to interpret my use of *he* or *him*, where applicable, in a gender-neutral manner. I have had the privilege to be engaged in the lives of thousands of people in service for the Lord. This has included persons in a wide range of ministry: international missions, North American churches, international churches, inner-city missions, Bible college and seminary students, and retired pastors.[5] The one thing that all of these have had in common is the experience of transition from one ministry to another. The reflections of this book have evolved over a long period.

This writing is an attempt to see the big picture, to make sense of the transition experience. It is an exploration to which I invite you in the hope that you will find answers

---

5   For those who would like from more information see Appendix: "About the Author."

personal to your own situation. Ministry is both poetry and prose, soaring and plodding. There is celebration and lamentation. Serving God is the greatest calling in the world, but it also presents enormous challenges. One must nurture others like a mother yet confront sin with the energy of a prophet. Success is defined in many different ways: growth, obedience, effectiveness, achievement of corporate or personal goals, etc. Failure may be defined in just as many different ways. Rather than focus on either success or failure, I invite you to look at transitioning from one ministry to another as a God-directed process. This will necessitate seeking some objectivity to balance one's personalizing of the experience.

Even if one has found fulfillment in a ministry, the transition from one opportunity to another will lead through adjustments with both negative and positive responses. Each experience is very personal, but there are commonalities as well as differences. If we move from one successful ministry to another, it will still involve dealing with the dynamics of transition. Recently, a pastor described his celebration of entering retirement as a good transition but an overwhelming experience of grief and loss. He grieved the loss of relationship with those amongst whom he ministered and those whom he had nurtured in their newfound faith. He felt misunderstood by those who had urged him to celebrate the new opportunity before him and those who now felt betrayed by his leaving. Others move from the painful experience of one ministry to another ministry. This is even more difficult than leaving a positive place of fulfilment. Walking with these *saints in service* has been an experience of much joy and suffering, exploring with them on the mountains and in the valleys the process of moving from ministry to ministry.

The Challenge of Transition

It is helpful to look at transition in terms of the stages one navigates in the experience. It will be different for each person; there are similarities common to everyone but also things that make each unique. First, let me provide a very brief overview by identifying five stages involved in transitioning from one ministry to another. These will be elaborated in succeeding chapters. The five stages are: The Starting Place, The Leaving, The In-Between Time, Entering New Ministry, and Belonging Again.

Each of these five stages may be explored in the following manner:

> Stage one: *The Starting Place* – A place of commitment that involves commitment, belonging, and intimacy.

> Stage two: *The Leaving* – Saying good-bye, which involves withdrawing, celebrating, and responding emotionally.

> Stage three: *The In-Between Time* – Experiencing the wilderness of transition, which involves loss of relationship, loss of role, and the anxiety of the unknown.

> Stage four: *Entering New Ministry* – A new beginning, which involves discovering who's who, finding one's place, and vulnerability.

> Stage five: *Belonging Again* – Renewing of vision, which involves bonding, experiencing mutuality, and security of place.[6]

---

6   Place is the community where we meet God with others. Paul Tournier, *A Place For You* (London: SCM Press, 1968)

Each person begins at a different place. Sometimes we are moving from an experience of fulfillment, or at other times leaving a place of pain, or a mixture of both. Without doubt one's motivation for moving will play a large role. The amount of time in one stage will impact the experience in that stage as well as our understanding of the other stages. One can readily see that all of these stages in the transition process will be influenced by personality as well as by very evident differences peculiar to each transition such as the age of the person, their capacity to deal with change, the presence of conflict, the need to interpret one's experience to others, the financial pressures, family dynamics, and the ages of children involved. I will provide six illustrations in which these differences can be seen.

REAL LIFE STORIES

The following stories are true in content but composite in nature and disguised so as not to duplicate any specific situation. Because of the common elements, it is hoped individuals will see some of their own experience in each of the stories. They illustrate the tough reality of transition from ministry to ministry regardless of the motivation to change location of ministry.

ONE: No Questions Permitted

George and his wife returned home one winter afternoon after a refreshing holiday. The following day the head elder called to arrange a visit. It seemed rather urgent. The pastor and elder met the next day. The elder's message was that the leadership of the church had decided the pastor should resign immediately. The following Sunday was to be his last day of ministry at the church. George gasped in shock at this news and requested that the issues be identified and discussed. He was informed that there could be no negotiation since the complaints had been given in a confidence that could not be breached. A severance package had been arranged, including counselling for George and his wife. George was bewildered, rejected, and confused. No explanation, no rational reason had been provided. He was left with only questions: What did he do wrong? Where was God? How could his ministry of six years come to this end? His wife was angry, as she felt her husband was being abused. He didn't deserve this. He had given his life to the church. Why this? There was no acknowledgement of their years of service. They were left with sadness, resentment, no resolution, ruminations filled with guilt, and anxiety about the future.

They sought professional counselling in the midst of their chaos. They were without status, were with limited resources, and had nowhere to turn for a quick solution to the financial uncertainty they faced. The good news is that God opened another door of ministry before they were in financial crises. Caution and questions about trust issues were faced and resolved, and a healthy ministry opportunity followed.

TWO: One Success Leads to Another Challenge

Philip was enjoying the blessings of God in effective ministry. After several years of evangelism and development, the congregation was cohesive, impacting their community and growing in spiritual maturity. Denominational leadership, witnessing Philip's effectiveness, approached him about the needs and opportunities in another growing subdivision in a large city. The challenge was great, and resources were available (both in people and financing) to launch a significant ministry in the new community. Philip, his wife, and his family earnestly prayed and experienced the call of God to respond to the challenge of this new ministry. They met and prayed with church leadership about the new opportunity and, with reluctance, the leadership communicated their support of Philip's decision to leave the church. Opportunities for celebration, closure, and farewell were arranged. The appreciation of many who had come to the Lord was expressed verbally and in writing. The church agreed to help in the new church planting, giving their blessing to the new project.

Once the decision to leave was made and the celebrations were over, Philip and Jane began to experience the sadness and loss of the relationships that had been so important over the years. In the new situation, it was difficult to know who to trust and to determine who was gifted to participate in leadership. The anxiety of *starting over* and the pressure of relocating their home and finding a temporary place of worship generated a sense of urgency and ambivalence. Long hours and intense planning stretched their spousal relationship in new ways. Jane was able to find part-time employment to supplement the lower income of a church planter. The blessing of God was upon the project, and within a short period, a new witness for Christ was established, and the church grew quickly as the new subdivision expanded.

THREE: "I No Longer Need You"

Sam was an associate pastor of a rather large church. The senior pastor embarked on doctoral studies while limiting his ministry to Sunday services. A large building expansion was entered into, in which Sam played the key role in planning and administration. The church continued to grow largely as a result of Sam's dynamic ministry and the leadership he developed among church members. Very shortly after completing his studies, the senior pastor asked for Sam's resignation, indicating he no longer felt he could work with him. The resignation was to be effective immediately, and his office was to be cleared in five days. Sam sought recourse from the elders, and they too confirmed the decision of the senior pastor, expressing that it was his right to select his team.

The devastation for Sam and his wife was overwhelming. Rejected, betrayed and unappreciated with no recourse, they were stunned and in disbelief that this could have happened. The denomination confirmed the power of the pastor. They felt betrayed by the leaders of both church and denomination. No opportunity was provided for appropriate good-byes to those with whom they had worked so closely. They felt lost and lonely but clung to each other. The children were too young to understand or participate but were aware something traumatic was happening. Nothing much is hidden from children. The children acted out their pain in unacceptable behaviour. The parents clung to their confidence in God's sovereignty and sought help from other pastors. Eventually they entered into another ministry in another province where they were welcomed into leadership in a not-for-profit organization.

FOUR: Family Issues in Transitions

Following theological training, Art experienced a clear and definite call to minister to youth. He and his wife evidenced the gifts and abilities to relate effectively to youth and had together rejoiced in God's blessing in youth ministry in two separate churches over a period of fifteen years. In his mid-thirties, Art became somewhat restless and felt the need for new challenges. Partly, he was weary of the hyperactivity and energized programing necessary for ministering effectively to youth. A call from another church raised the possibility of moving from youth ministry to an associate pastor role that would include ministry to adults with some opportunity to preach. The call was accepted, but the opportunity for ministry to adults and for preaching the Word did not materialize. Medical complications in Art's family required the proximity of specialists in medicine.

Moving was difficult to contemplate in the event that this need could not be met. Further negotiation with church leadership did not create the opportunities desired. Art began to question whether his sense of call was motivated by wrong desires. He became increasingly discouraged and quite depressed, which increased his internal struggles. Where was God in all of this? Should he submit to the leadership where he was located? Would they find comparable medical support elsewhere? Would a much needed employment opportunity be found for his wife? There were more questions than answers.

FIVE: Moral Failure, Overload, and Burnout

Eric, after successfully completing seminary training during which he gained some pastoral experience, went on to two fruitful pastorates in small to moderate- sized western cities. He was invited to join a team of three other pastors (a lead pastor, youth pastor, and music pastor) in a thriving, expanding church community. After five years, two of the pastors became involved in struggles within their families. Moral failure resulted in both of those pastors leaving the church. Discouraged, the third pastor left. Eric continued trying to bring healing to the congregation. He was enabled to carry on due to a strong sense of call and his commitment to the principle that "if I work harder I will succeed with the Lord's blessing."

His sense of responsibility and duty carried him, although with rather negative responses from his family. The children felt they had essentially lost a father and that the blatant immorality of the other pastors disproved Christianity's validity. The children became confused and rejected all relationship with Christianity. He carried the entire ministry for a couple of years until a new lead pastor was identified and called. The new pastor asked Eric to continue. After eighteen months, the new pastor informed Eric that he was no longer needed or wanted, and his resignation was requested immediately. The elders, when consulted, supported the new pastor's freedom to choose his own team.

Eric left with deep pain and a strong sense of rejection and failure. He was encouraged by denominational leadership to leave quietly. He took his burnt-out and abused self into another impossible challenge of ministry in a different denomination. That pastorate became a disaster largely because of circumstances beyond his control. However, contributing factors were the depression, exhaustion, spiritual dryness and sense of failure brought forward from the previous situation. Eric consulted other pastors and denominational leaders about his sense of spiritual dryness and feelings that God had abandoned him. Sermon preparation became a labour of failure. Denominational leadership counselled him to use the sermons of others who granted permission. This worked for a while but left Eric guilty and confused as to the rightness of such a practice.

The unfinished business of the previous rejection and a sense of powerlessness in the present increased his sense of failure and plunged Eric into further depression. There appeared to be no resolution.

SIX: This Is Not Me

Julio was raised in a Christian home and was heavily involved in athletic activity in which he excelled. As a child he dreamed of being a professional soccer player, and he was good. His father was a successful businessman who loved nothing better than leading other people to faith in Christ. At a young age, Dad said, "Julio, you are going to be a preacher. You have the gifts to be a pastor, and God is calling you." The confidence of his father swelled in Julio's heart. He worked hard at school subjects, even though his heart was in his successful soccer exploits. The family moved a long way from their original home to a community where there was no opportunity for soccer.

Finishing secondary school, it seemed natural for Julio to go to Bible College where he did well academically but not so well socially. Perseverance saw him through to graduation. He was placed in youth work. Opportunities increased, and he moved to adult ministries and eventually into the pastorate as an associate. The churches in which he served were very legalistic, and the pastors under whom he served were autocratic and domineering. When the opportunity came to go solo, he jumped at it. With no training in leadership or conflict management, he struggled with a few dominant businessmen in the congregation who found fulfillment in controlling the congregation both with influence and financial coercion. Being unable to cope with assertive and aggressive individuals, Julio felt trampled, frustrated, and devoid of influence. Suppressed anger issued in depression and exhaustion. Denominational leadership was consulted, and these men supported the influencers in the congregation, suggesting that Julio go quietly. He did. He resigned with a heavy burden of failure and guilt.

Exploration of his abilities and gifts while in professional counselling led him to conclude that fulfilling the dream of his father was not, in fact, God's calling for him. The relief was real, but the uncertainty of the future generated more anxiety. Julio's story is unfinished. He seeks God for the next chapter in his life.

Summary Observations

These stories provide some perspective for looking into the process of transition. No one story can represent the diversity of experience and the interplay between an individual, a family, a congregation, and a community when a change in ministry occurs.

After many years of journeying with individuals in transition, I have tried to identify the range of common experiences met by a diversity of ministering persons. This has been an attempt to summarize and process the life stories of these pastors. The journey of these people was sacred and should be handled with care. Many expressed a wish that others could benefit from their trials. The stories I have told do not adequately recount their emotional response, nor do these stories represent all of the issues raised by transition in ministry, but they are representative. On reflection I wrote a poem trying to capture what I heard from them. With some hesitation, I share with you the sense of pain, confusion, rejection, anger, and loss that was the experience of many. My hope is that you will get in touch with their pain and perhaps find words for your own.

I Listened to Pain

Portions of the past
Depressed, pushed down,
Stuffed deep,
Sealed in silence.
Pain pushed to oblivion.

Yet, bubbling, boiling,
Building pressure,
Crouched to spring,
Disguised in a confusion
Of distorted emotions.

Yet, nowhere to turn but inward.
Steel-cold eyes unfocused
In tight intensity, while thoughts
Repeating patterns of self-blame,
Self-hate, underserved but unavoidable.

Anger screamed in silence
Shattering the body
With tremors of emotion.
Body friend becomes body enemy.

Pain shouted silently
Through body language in vain tremblings,
Clenched fists, thin lips, knotted stomach.
Eyes crying dry tears
Burning with unblinking stares.

Interacting with pastors in transition has reminded me often of Psalm 22, where we read of the suffering servant: "God, God...my great God! Why did you dump me miles from nowhere? Doubled up in pain, I call to God all the day long."[7] It requires great courage to wrestle with the issues related to transition. It is also most helpful to have others alongside because this river is not easily crossed alone.

An Invitation to Reflection

It is rare that a pastor in North America serves in only one church for his entire vocational career. Those engaged in overseas ministry will move from one culture to another and, in many cases, one ministry to another while continuing to serve with the same organization or denomination. One thing that is common to both homeland and overseas ministry is the experience of moving from one location to another. The process of transition is a challenging one and has a greater impact than is understood by most people. It means relocation, resettlement, refocusing, and renewing of opportunities and challenges. The impact is dramatic and in many cases traumatic. The accumulated effects of transition lead to adjustments that have long-term consequences.

On the other hand, the crises experienced in transition create an opportunity for one to explore and understand oneself and the vocational ministry to which one is called. Exploration and understanding of this process may be a creative opportunity to clarify and renew one's call and commitment. It may be an opportunity to start again, to correct or revise one's previous expression of ministry. I want you to explore

---

[7] Psalm 22:1-2 (MSG)

and understand your experiences of transition. Exploration requires that we open the windows of our minds to let the breeze of fresh evidence blow away the flimsy cobwebs of unknowing. Openness leads to new discovery and new vistas of character growth in the inner man. It also facilitates a clearer understanding of ministry and leadership.

Many times transition in ministry can result in much pain, anger, turmoil, and confusion. The experience of transition must be embraced for us to gain the learning potential that lies within it. What follows will provide an opportunity to change the grief and pain of transition into a transformed ministry. In this book, transition is viewed as an opportunity for a reflective pause wherein to look at ministry and our role in it. Learning from one's past ministry so as to discover changes for future ministry may turn out to be a most valuable opportunity. It may enable us to change *my story* of past ministry into *God's story* and lead toward a renewed commitment in vocation, which is the rationale for the process and structure of this book.

A Reflective Pause Defined

Reflecting on our experience of transition in ministry may help us to discover the presence of God in those transitions, whether they have been joyful or painful. Many have come to view transition as a creative opportunity for their revision and understanding of ministry as well as an opportunity to explore self-understanding. Our discussion will identify some foundational principles that may assist to inhibit the natural outcomes of pressure in ministry.

Exploring ministry in the light of one's experience is not for the purpose of revising of our doctrine; instead, it seeks

Chapter 1: The Challenge of Changing Ministries

to understand the practice of ministry and our own personal experience along our career path in serving God. A reflective pause is a case of setting aside sufficient time to reflect on the experience of transition. To be effective this requires that we do so in a setting conducive to quiet reflection, with openness of heart and mind to hear what God desires to teach us through the experience. Our hearts must be hospitable to the Spirit's instruction. It is usually most effective to follow a carefully designed structure and enter into the experience with some guidance by another objective and caring person. This can be a great and glorious adventure that we are invited into by the grace of God.

It is my prayer that you find his grace sufficient in your calling. The stages through which pastors pass in the experience of transition will be discussed in chapters three and four.

> Remember these things, O Jacob,
> for you are my servant, O Israel.
> I have made you, you are my servant;
> O Israel, I will not forget you.
>
> Isaiah 44:21

Questions for Reflection:

How many transitions in ministry have I experienced? Where did the motivation for these transitions originate? Were they more positive or negative as an experience in ministry? What was the impact on spouse, family or future ministry? More benefit will result if you record your reflections and evaluate any changes in perception as you move through succeeding chapters.

Chapter Two

Pastors in Transition

> You're blessed when you feel you've lost
> what is most dear to you.
> Only then can you be embraced
> by the One most dear to you.
>
> Beatitudes (MSG)

The analogy of traversing a river has been used to provide a picture of pastors in transition. There are many ways to cross a river. Interacting with many pastors moving from one ministry to another has convinced me that the river they are crossing is often treacherous and the means are rather primitive. This has been happening for many years and happens frequently in the careers of most pastors, yet strangely it has not received the attention it deserves. I know of no research that has identified the number of times each pastor is likely to transition from one ministry to another. Many suggested pastorates rarely extend much beyond four years. If this is the case, over a period of fifty years transition would occur a dozen times. These chapters will offer ways to identify the experience in stages.

It must be acknowledged that transitioning is quite different each time and different for each individual. However, the differences do not preclude a commonality of elements. Continuing with my analogy of crossing a river, I would observe there are many ways to navigate the river. The characteristics of each river will be different. Some rivers are quiet and idyllic, while others are raging torrents. Some are shallow, and some are wide. Having canoed in Northern Ontario, I can assure you that launching and off-loading is more or less difficult depending on the shoreline. Shores may be sandy, rocky, rugged, or steep, and this will have an impact on how one can launch from one to the other. Rarely would the transition of a pastor be so easy as flying over the river or crossing on a bridge. A few are easily accomplished, but they are the exceptions.

The majority of transitions from the shore of one ministry to another are like going through the river, crossing by rowboat, car ferry, cable ferry, or maybe by life raft. Some of these crossings are deeply personal, engaging, traumatic, and a great deal more difficult. You may choose any one of these means of crossing as an apt analogy for your experience. My intention is to look at the process of crossing as occurring in the five stages previously mentioned. We will look at each stage in the next few chapters and seek to understand them.

DIMENSIONS AND STAGES OF TRANSITION

Pastoral transition is the movement of a pastor from a place of involvement through the in-between stage to re-engagement:

The Starting Place (*Breaking Camp*)

The Leaving (*Departing from Shore*)

The In-Between Time (*The Crossing*)

Entering New Ministry (*Landing on the Other Shore*)

Belonging Again (*Setting up Camp*)

Let's try to understand the experience of a person as they progress through these five stages. It is necessary to consider each stage from different perspectives. These perspectives may be defined as one's *social posture*, one's *social status*, and one's *emotional response*. As we move forward in seeking to understand transition, we will look at each of the five stages from these three perspectives. By *social posture* we are referring to the position, role, or function the person has with their accompanying responsibility and authority. By *social status* we mean the standing, significance, or place of respect commensurate with the office the person holds. *Emotional response* identifies the affective response of the person as they relate to the opportunities and challenges of their experience in each stage. The five stages will lead to alterations in one's social posture, social status, and emotional experience. This is illustrated in the diagram on page 27.

The experience of pastors over their career path usually involves engagement with several churches. The ministry of a missionary frequently demands not only transition from culture to culture, but also change from one role in ministry to another role. Quite often Christian leaders of charitable organizations will also serve in more than one organization. There are similarities between all of these transitions. This is a time of anxiety, involving worry, re-evaluation, and often disappointment. For some, the transition will be from one church to another. For others it may be from youth pastor to lead pastor or from one level in an organization to another level. In other cases, it may be an outcome of chronology; that is, as pastors mature they may desire a change in ministry or a different focus in ministry to accommodate their own natural, developmental changes. Change in ministry location or responsibility leads to a range of emotional responses, social change, family and location change, and often changes in philosophy of ministry for various reasons.

Change is integral to the transitory nature of ministry. The human capacity for anticipation often leads to the initiation of change, and our creativity enables a responsiveness to change brought upon us by others. Both of these stretch our capacity. Sometimes we fear change. Perhaps a more creative response is to embrace change through faith in the Sovereign God. Faith is the most effective pathway with which to explore change.

Illustrating the Experience

The stories provided in the first chapter illustrate this point. It may be helpful to go back to those six stories and think of them in terms of the stages and of the three perspectives indicated. Let me give a personal illustration. I have transitioned from one ministry to another a number of times. Early on, I was commissioned to pioneer three new churches. The first two commissions were short lived due to education and health concerns. Leaving each was a different experience. The first transition was precipitated because of illness, the extensive travel required, and a need to complete my theological training. My depth of grief, loss, and disappointment was compounded by pneumonia. My second was different in that the church was established, and there was a sense of completion and celebration. However, these were coupled with strong bereavement: the congregation wanted me to continue, but the miles to travel between the church and the seminary made that impossible.

My third transition was to leave a church my wife and I had pioneered and pastored for four years. Leaving was necessitated by my desire for further education. That was a time of celebration but also one of questioning. Mentors and peers questioned my motivation for pursuing further studies. They communicated their fear that I would lose my passion for pastoral ministry. I felt the loneliness of rejection. Breaking the bonds that had developed within the congregation and its leadership was very painful. Financial concerns were also pressing, for my wife and I had two children and few resources. In each case, the ministry experience was unique; the shore, the crossing and the landing were all quite different. Each stage brought challenge and change.

THE TURMOIL OF CHANGE

Transitions in ministry are fraught with strong emotions, both positive and negative. The termination of a vision, the loss of relationships, changing roles, and severing important associations will be part of the experience. Frequently, there are negative elements that include the sense of rejection, betrayal, anger, and frustration over unresolved issues. Even when there has been an obvious call of God and a project is completed with celebration, there are mixed emotions that generate turmoil. Not the least of factors involved is the impact of the transition on one's spouse and family. Then there is the necessity of physical relocation. In the real experience of transition, one's faith does not eliminate a flurry of normal human responses. One must not deny the pain but rather embrace it with God.

It is this experience of transition that I wish to explore with you. There may be pain in looking at your particular transitioning experience; however, resolution in God's grace is a very distinct and achievable option. Your pain will be as real as your touch with life's emotions and the self-awareness that comes as you explore your full response to your experience in openness before God. The goal is that your times of transition serve as an opportunity for you to become intimate with God and find what he desires to teach through this challenge. It is said of Noah as he built the ark (which did not make sense to anyone around him), "Noah became intimate with God."[8] It is not difficult to imagine that this intimacy came in the midst of what was a trying time that tested his faith.

When my oldest grandson was six years of age, he experienced a moment of inspiration. We were saying good-bye and giving the usual hugs when he said, "Let's have an everybody hug!" When we are in transition, we need an everybody hug including the Holy Spirit, the Father, Jesus, and loved ones while we embrace the pain of transition. May this be your discovery as you navigate pastoral transitions!

Exploring an Understanding of Transition

Pastoral transition involves moving from one place of involvement through the *in-between* stage toward re-engagement. There are several levels of response to each of these stages. To explore one's personal passage, it helps to consider one's social posture, social status, and emotional response in each stage of transition. We have noted that pastors, over their career path, are usually engaged with several churches. The life of a missionary frequently demands not only transition from culture to culture but also change from one role in ministry to another. For some the transition will be from one church to another. For others it may be from youth pastor to lead pastor. In other cases, it may be an outcome of chronology; that is, as pastors mature they may desire a change in ministry, or a ministry with a different focus.

---

8 Genesis 6:9 (MSG)

There may be pain in looking at your particular time of transition. Let me reiterate what was stated earlier. Resolution in God's grace is a very distinct and achievable option. Your pain will be as real as your touch with life in the self-awareness that comes as you explore your full response to your transition in openness before God. Your healing will be as real and complete as your touch with God and His grace to you.

My involvement in a research group with several other professionals and representatives from eight different mission organizations over a period of ten years has shaped my thinking and clarified my perspectives on the transition of those who serve in other cultures. This research focused on the lives of youth and families to the impact of cross-cultural ministry relationally, spiritually, emotionally, and organizationally. Much of this research has been reported at the Mental Health and Missions conference held annually for over thirty years. This conference has grown to engage well over two hundred participants from health professions and from a great many mission organizations. My wife and I participated for twenty-five years and benefited much from the interaction with those who provide care for pastors and missionaries serving cross-culturally.

Two of my personal friends, David C. Pollock and Ruth E. Van Reken, have expanded our understanding of the transition experience of third-culture kids (i.e. the children of missionaries) and their parents.[9] Pollock, who served on the research group mentioned earlier, developed a descriptive outline of the

---

9   Pollock, David C. & Van Reken, Ruth E. (2001) *Third Culture Kids*, (Yarmouth,MN: Intercultural Press) Third Culture Kids was the term created to identify the experience of children who being raised in other cultures grew up with aspects of the host culture incorporated into their experience as well as the culture of their parents. They, essentially, developed a *third culture* that was distinct from that of both parents and the host culture.

experience of transition among missionaries from the perspective of social posture, social status, psychological experience, and time orientation. With Pollock's permission, I used his perspective to develop an understandable way to describe the transition experience of pastors and other Christian leaders.

Over a time line, whether days or months, people move from their present ministry to their future ministry passing through a no-man's land of transition. This in-between place (the crossing of the river) between ministries is the heart of transition. However, the nature of that experience is determined by what preceded and what follows it. As one approaches their departure from a ministry, a distancing from those with whom they have been involved will occur. The anticipation of change activates this moving away from others. This disengagement is normal and often completely unconscious. The time between ministries can be a time of chaos and confusion. Entering a new ministry in a new context triggers a response of tentative engagement and a time of adjustment to the new situation. People will move through these stages at different speeds and with differing degrees of anxiety, depending on many factors.

Let me reiterate: an individual pastor's experience of leaving one ministry and entering another happens several times over their lifetime. This is the norm. It is also important to look at the experience between ministries as part of the transition. The leaving of one ministry, the time between ministries, and the entering of a new opportunity may be unsettling and traumatic. This will vary from person to person due to a multitude of different factors.

THE TRANSITION EXPERIENCE OF PASTORS
(Glenn C. Taylor)[10]

Dimensions of Experience	Starting Place: Place of Commitment	The Leaving: Saying Good-bye	In-Between Time: Experiencing Wilderness	Entering: New Beginnings	Belonging: Renewal of Vision
Social Posture	Committed Responsible Dutiful Concerned	Withdrawing Loosen Ties Disengage Withdraw	Loss of Relationships Isolation Self-defense	Who's who Superficial Uncertain trust Finding Partners	Committed Bonding Belonging Visioning
Social Status	Belonging Part of Group Reputation Respect Knowing/Known	Farewells Closure Celebration Attention Recognition	Loss of Role Loss of Community Time without Use Unknown	Introductions Marginal Depth of Relationship Expectations Unknown	Position Respect Part of Community Known
Emotional Responses	Intimacy Bonded with others Secure Affirmed	Sadness Rejection Guilt Resentment Anger	Anxiety of the Unknown Grief of loss Stress and anger symptoms	Anxiety of Expectations Fear Guarded Ambivalent	Intimacy Security of Place Affirmed Bonded with others

The illustrations in the first chapter bear this out. Each story illustrates a different experience of transition. The motivations and outcomes of transition vary with each situation.

The decision to leave one's ministry will be different in a multi-staff church than when one is the sole pastor. The relationship between pastor and other leaders (elders, deacons, management team, and advisory team) will have a great impact.

One of the factors that influence transition is the degree to which the leadership of the church are guided by the processes practiced in our secular culture rather than by biblical principles. Church leaders who are in executive or leadership roles in the secular community all too often import

---

10   Adapted from early work by David C. Pollock.

the procedures they use in their secular employment into relationships in their church function. In our secular culture, many processes that apply to the employer-employee relationship are inappropriate for a church context. For example, a business is a profit-driven corporation with production expectations necessary to its success. These expectations of necessity incorporate dimensions of an adversarial nature because of the competing interest of the different parties, and may be increased by unionization or the desire for larger profits for different interest groups. It is problematic to define the pastor-church relationship in terms of employer-employee terminology. Ministry should not be defined as work or employment. Rather, it is best defined as a means to the fulfillment of one's calling by God.

Ministry creates the opportunity for me to enter into the work of God in the lives of people. Hierarchical analogies implied in the relationship do not fit. Although the pastor serves the community of faith, his primary calling is from God. He has neither the authority to dictate nor should he be in a place of subservience to church leadership. The covenantal relationship must be defined biblically, and our cultural categories are an inadequate source of information and direction.

Within a Christian church, all competing interests are subject to a pursuit of the will of God and conformity to the mind and behaviour of Christ in all community relationships. Procedures of dismissal in a secular context have limited value when considered in a Christian community. Much pain is generated in churches by the application of procedures appropriate to a corporation that are not appropriate to a community of faith.

This common problem is an outcome of failure on the part of denominations and pastors to clearly train church leaders in biblical patterns of leadership. The replication of secular policies and practices in a church context leads to much conflict. Frequently, those elected to spiritual leadership in the church are not gifted or trained to deal with conflict in a manner consistent with biblical guidelines. The result is that adversarial patterns in our culture are imported into church culture. Paul the Apostle found that the church at Corinth was seeking to resolve issues with secular processes.[11] It is necessary to function within cultural expectations when dismissing a pastor or considering severance. However, the differences between a pastor's role and that of a corporation employee are great.

Additionally, the redemptive nature of the community of faith must express itself in any of these actions. We must follow the principles of Scripture rather than the defensive and protective policies applied in our secular society. The Scriptures are abundantly clear as to the manner in which we are to deal with our differences.[12] Some pastors who are dismissed with cause are provided for by their churches with adequate severance consideration. Others, who have served faithfully for many years and are released into retirement, have received no severance. There is considerable variance from denomination to denomination as to how churches or pastors contribute to retirement funds. It is my observation that church leadership will frequently apply secular principles to dealing with conflict and show no interest in a generosity of retirement severance when dealing with pastors who have served well. One pastor

---

11 1 Corinthians 6:1-11

12 It is not my purpose here to discuss conflict in the church but rather to understand the experience of transition. I will suggest one very good book. Barthel & Edling, *Redeeming Church Conflict*, (Grand Rapids,MI: Baker Books, 2012)

observed, "I would have been treated more fairly if I had given them cause to fire me, rather than quietly moving on."

My desire in addressing the transition of pastors is to encourage an open dialogue with all of the participants in the process. An approach that could honour the Lord would bring great benefit to all involved.

OUTCOMES OF TRANSITION

Transition most often involves financial stress and the impact of relocation including anxiety about the education and (in some cases), medical care of family members. Individuals frequently engage in a painful process of self-examination and self-re-crimination, or they experience concern about the judgement of others and the impact on peer relationships among their pastoral friends. Add to these the necessity of finding another opportunity for the ministry, if one feels called to continue. At this point, there is often a consideration of dropping out. It would be my expectation that research would see a correlation between transition and pastors leaving the ministry. The selection process often leaves pastors feeling that they are competing with other pastors for the call of a church. The anxiety of finding God's will, while at the same time being in need of healing, is very real for many. It is my serious concern that inadequate attention to pastors going through transition leads to the loss of many in Christian service and to great instability in churches. Additionally, it is important to understand the impact that we have in our community by the way in which we deal with the transition of pastors.

In cross-cultural missions much more attention has been given to the impact of transition on personnel and families. There has been a greater openness on the part of missionaries to address the dynamics of transition. This is because in the cross-cultural setting, the outcomes are sometimes more dramatic and not so readily hidden. Also, there has been much more research and activity focused on the care of missionary personnel. My involvement with both pastors and missionaries has led me to believe that the transition experience is very similar for each regardless of the differences and uniqueness of these two aspects of ministry.

> Fear not, for I have redeemed you;
> I have summoned you by name; you are mine.
> When you pass through the waters, I will be with you;
> and when you pass through the rivers, they will not sweep over you…
> For I am the Lord, your God, the Holy One of Israel, your Savior.
>
> Isaiah 43:1-3

QUESTIONS FOR REFLECTION

Can you separate the stages in your transitions? Identify the losses with respect to social posture, social status. What feelings predominated? Own loses with integrity by naming them. What were the most pressing issues for you as you became aware that a transition was about to occur? The most common ones are family, education and care of children, finance, moving, and a sense of failure. You may want to go back to the illustration in chapter one to identify these elements more clearly.

Chapter Three

The Transition Experience

> You're blessed when you're at the end of your rope.
> With less of you, there is more of God and his rule.
>
> Beatitudes (MSG)

In the last chapter, the transition experience was described as consisting of five stages: *The Starting Place, The Leaving, The In-Between Time, Entering New Ministry,* and *Belonging Again*. In this chapter, we will look at the first three stages in more detail. The fourth and fifth stage will be discussed in chapters six through nine.

Obviously, people move through these stages on different time lines and with differing degrees of anxiety. The outcomes experienced in each stage will depend on many variables, including the personal functioning of the individual. We each respond out of who we are and our understanding of God's involvement in our lives. The model has helped many to navigate the experience of transition. Creating a reflective pause wherein one explores their transition can have great rewards.

Let's begin at the beginning, that is, *The Starting Place*. Whatever has led to the decision to terminate ministry, understanding the qualities and characteristics of that place will determine what follows. Bear in mind that each stage will involve understanding from the perspective of social posture, social status, and emotional responses. A comprehensive picture will emerge only as we grasp the meaning of the experience from these dimensions. This is the launching pad or to use the analogy introduced earlier, it is one's camping place, and breaking camp is the place from which transition begins.

THE STARTING PLACE

A church pastor will have responsibilities and duties that entail both obligation and commitment. This is his social posture as defined in chapter two and which can be placed in the larger picture in the diagram on page 8 of that chapter. His sense of belonging is enhanced by his commitment along with leadership, reputation, respect, and position. The pastoral role as pictured in the New Testament with its focus on teaching and nurturing, naturally leads to close bonding with people. The satisfaction of coming to know others intimately in times of stress and times of joy will have been an important part of the experience. Leadership and public involvement leads to the pastor being known both in the church and the local community. The longer one experiences such commitment, belonging, and intimacy, the greater the degree of bonding. This is what is meant by social status and emotional response. If the pastor experiences this depth of commitment and bonding it is likely to be reciprocated by members of the congregation with mutual responsiveness, respect, and affirmation. Also, one's sense of security will increase. If these qualities have been a part of the ministry experience, the *camp* will have had many pleasurable moments in spite of any tensions. It will have been a comfortable place to be. Perhaps there were many challenges, but if on the whole one saw God at work in one's ministry, one will have experienced a sense of belonging.

Some pastors by nature are more reserved, less extroverted, and thus may not become intimately engaged with those whom they serve. Many things may contribute to a pastor being more aloof from their church community. Personality may evoke a reticence to become close to others. Previous experience of pain in relationships, or a philosophy of leadership that places the leader apart from those being led, may also lead to distancing in relationships. Some pastors have a sense of professionalism and a philosophy of ministry that suggests they must not get too close to the people they serve.

Regardless of differing relationships of pastors to their church communities most of the characteristics described as being part of *The Starting Place* will apply. As indicated in the diagram on page 8, chapter 2, the pastor in his commitment to ministry will evidence the *social posture, social status* and *emotional responses* indicated. *The Starting Place* will be characterized by commitment, responsibility, duty, and concern for the congregation. The pastor will experience a sense of belonging, being part of the in-group, respect, reputation and a place of knowing and being known. There will be a development of intimacy and bonding that will provide affirmation and security. Humans were created for community and, each in our own way find the comfort of community in our association with others. The opportunity to have significant input into the lives of others quite naturally leads to these responses. A minority may, as a result of past experience, restrain themselves from such engagement. This will be true of only a very small minority, but if this happens, it will be contributed to largely by the past experience of the church.

Churches that have had difficult experiences with previous pastors are likely to withhold themselves from becoming too personally involved with a new pastor. If one follows the history of a church it will become evident that churches tend to replicate their experience with pastors. In addition to the history of the church, the social environment and the nature of the community in which the church is located will have an impact.

The ecclesiology of the denomination and the authority structures that impact pastoral placement are important. Some denominations have a policy of short-term ministry and move pastors every three to four years. Others with a hierarchical approach may move individuals for political reasons. This may result from individuals within the community exercising control over the church and inappropriately finding their own needs met through their dominance. A few adversarial individuals in a church can affect a church for generations. One church congregation experienced similar difficulties with six of nine pastors over its forty-year history. It is a major task to change such a culture when it has become imbedded in a church. The level of spiritual maturity represented in the congregation will significantly impact the relationship between pastor and people.

We must also recognize the family relationships of the pastor, the nature of the spousal relationship, the age and number of children, and related family dynamics. Length of pastorate, the degree of identification of the pastor with the congregation, and the expectations of longevity on the part of both pastor and church will influence their relationship. Because the experience of each pastor is different, generalizations never completely fit one's own personal experience, for every pastor's situation is unique. However, these variables can be identified and understood in the context of each situation.

The experience of a favourable involvement is what both pastor and church anticipate. The development of their relationship usually begins with a strong desire to be all God wishes the church to be. The pastor who experiences such an engagement with a congregation will be motivated to serve the Lord with zeal. Most people will celebrate with joy and acceptance, a union of pastor and congregation that leads to fulfilling ministry.

A full understanding of the nature of *The Starting Place* is essential for understanding the significance of transition to a new place of service. Failure to understand the personal meaning found in one's place of service or to minimize its significance in one's life not only robs one of much joy but makes it impossible to deal with the losses associated with leaving. One cannot assess the significance of change without understanding the depth of one's prior experience and its importance to one's identity.

There is a biblical emphasis on remembering the past. Looking to the past reminds us of the presence of God in his grace, love, and faithfulness, if we focus on what he has accomplished in our ministry. To acknowledge the grace of God in one's ministry and the giftedness we have demonstrated in ministry is not an act of pride but rather an act of praise. To celebrate the positive experiences in one's ministry and to acknowledge one's role in it, as instruments in God's hand, is an act of thanksgiving. There is a difference between looking to the past to analyse it and looking to the past to celebrate God's grace and blessing in all that we experienced. We also look to the past for the lessons God desired to teach us. It is often only in retrospect that we learn what he intended for us to learn.

As he was preparing to leave his disciples, Jesus observed on at least two occasions that much could be learned by looking back upon an experience that might not have made much sense at the time. "You do not realize now what I am doing, but later you will understand." And again, "I am telling you now before it happens so that when it does happen you will believe that I am He."[13] Earlier, in discussing the Triumphal entry into Jerusalem, John states, "At first the disciples did not understand all of this."[14] It is difficult to understand experience in the existential moment but later, with further information, insight, objectivity, and the leading of the Spirit of God, we can learn much. Retrospective analysis, unless guided by wisdom from above, may often lead to paralysis. In looking to the past, we want to see the hand of God. We must not let our pain obliterate our vision of God's presence in our ministry. A clear understanding of what our engagement in ministry means to us will enable us to achieve a clearer understanding of our transition experience.

A missionary letter recently spoke of "peephole driving." This evoked a memory for me. One cold winter morning while driving to university, someone slammed into my car. The driver exclaimed, "I couldn't see you!" The investigating police officer said he had fifteen percent vision through the ice that covered his windshield. He had been peephole driving! Often in looking at our past we use peephole vision, which often means looking through the limitation of pain, discouragement, and anxiety. It is helpful to broaden our vision both backward and forward. We need a clear vision of where we have come from and where we are going. Such clarity comes through letting the Spirit of God clear away the ice so that we may clearly see the mind of God. Reason alone does not sustain. The mystery of God in our lives of ministry

---

13   John 13:7, 20
14   John 12:16

requires an open heart to the wind of the Spirit if we are to grasp the action of God in faith.

The Wounds of God

> God only wounds that he may heal.
> He breaks that he may mend
> In his healing and mending,
> We become well and whole;
> Strengthened, to walk strong and tall.

Isaiah, the prophet, speaks of a time "when the Lord binds up the bruises of his people and heals the wounds he inflicted" (30:26).

The Leaving

One's motivations for leaving a ministry are very difficult to discern especially to the individual in the midst of transition. The overt conditions or interactions that motivate change are more readily agreed upon. It is less helpful to focus on motivations than to pay attention to the relational interactions that led to the decision. For this reason, my focus is not to try to analyse the reason for leaving but to focus on more tangible factors. These range over a broad spectrum. It is most helpful to focus on the most concrete factors first. The place to begin is with the objective facts and immediately definable process experienced. This leads to increasing objectivity and reducing the distortions that come from otherwise beginning with feelings. The initiating elements may be conflict, personal factors, family concerns, moral failure, loss of vision, leadership differences or a multitude of other possibilities.

Pastors in Transition

My interest is to explore the experience of leaving as it is lived by the pastor and his family. To focus on the more subjective elements of the disengagement often leads to defensiveness, assignment of blame, accusations or judgments that are beyond our capacity to make. A better route is to pursue understanding of the personal experience of the pastor and his family.

Not all terminations are an outcome of problems. Some are intentionally planned by authorities in one's denomination. Some occur due to a conviction of God's leading. Then again, the cause for leaving may not always be clear. The purpose is to understand what has been experienced rather than to express judgement or to analyse motives.

The life of Jesus and his disciples evidence another important consideration. Jesus's departure was a necessary ending, pre-planned and predicted throughout God's revelation of himself in the Old Testament. Sometimes, the leaving of a pastor is a necessary ending. This concept is elaborated on by Henry Cloud and applied to corporate and business relationships.[15] Understanding one's experience in transition may lead to the discovery that the ending was necessary to the fulfillment of God's purpose. God desires our growth and learning through all the experiences he permits or brings into our lives. It is often only in retrospect that we can conclude that our experience of leaving was, in fact, a necessary ending from God's perspective. We need to be clear that necessary endings bring with them the dynamics of loss, grief, and all the experiences that are a part of the *In-Between* stage.

Let me apply my analogy. *Leaving* is departing from camp, which involves packing up and entering the boat to cross the river to another place. The more care taken in

---

15   Henry Cloud, *Necessary Endings*, (New York, NY: Harper-Collins, 2012)

packing up camp, the easier the crossing. The more tidiness we leave behind, the more pleasant the place will be for the next camper. The more carefully we pack our gear the easier it will be to unpack at the next stop in our journey. This is the imagery of getting into a canoe and crossing the river of transition. How well we leave this shore will be influenced by how well we have prepared our leaving and the amount of baggage we take with us. How neatly we can pack makes stowing our cargo more efficient. This contributes to stability in the crossing. Tragically, some are forced to leave quickly and have little opportunity for appropriate leaving. With this imagery in mind, let's consider leaving a place of ministry.

Whether a decision to move is anticipated, dictated or initiated by oneself there is a distancing that occurs between the pastor and the church family. People may not be conscious of this distancing. It is a normal protective action, and it will occur regardless of how the change came about. There will be evidence of withdrawal on the part of pastor, leadership, and congregation. Relinquishing of roles and responsibility by both pastor and people will begin to occur. A decision that is mutual and agreeable is usually followed by celebration. Otherwise, the outcome will involve sentiments of rejection, resentment, sadness, and guilt.

When a pastor leaves, churches wrestle with almost as many different responses as there are people involved. We each experience separation in different ways. Some people may withdraw to have time to process their experience; others will spontaneously erupt whether in joy, sorrow, anger or grief. Some will be very rational and immediately begin to project how the experience has impacted them or the community as a whole. When any dramatic event occurs, it challenges the status quo and shakes relationships at their core. Different reactions add to already significant tension. Often the question is, "Why don't others respond like me? Is there something wrong with me or them?" Leadership must be prepared to acknowledge a variety of responses and to affirm the diversity in people's experiences. Leadership through this process is crucial.

When a pastor is required to leave by reason of moral failure or other serious issues, the leadership frequently falls to the elders or deacons. These leaders need to be cared for as well as the pastor. One such elder came to me for counselling. The burden he was expected to bear in the midst of tensions between pastor and people and between various members of the congregation led to depression and anxiety. He broke under the pressure. Post-Traumatic Stress Disorder (PTSD) was experienced with significant loss of health. He had been elected as a gifted spiritual leader and had evidenced many gifts in caring for people. However, he was not prepared for conflict management. This scenario is frequently duplicated when pastors leave out of necessity, and many churches do not recover from this trauma.

In one church where the pastor was asked to leave because of moral failure, trauma continued for many years. The pastor moved on and sought healing and forgiveness. The church leadership continued to regurgitate the experience to the destruction of the church as a congregation and to the loss of its effectiveness in the community. When it was suggested that the leadership should consider looking in the mirror of their own hearts to assess their contribution to the pastor's moral failure, they reacted with anger. It was easier for them to blame than to explore their own culpability. The history of that church was littered with pastors who had problems for which the leadership assumed no responsibility. Locked in this response, they proceeded to decline into ineffectiveness in their community. Reconciliation is the most desirable option and requires repentance and forgiveness on the part of everyone.

There must come a time to let go and leave with the Lord what cannot be resolved. In our human experience not all issues are resolvable. Such issues may lead to a necessary ending. The inconsistency and variability of human response is well illustrated in the case of Moses. The response of Israel to the redemptive love of God (in rescuing them from the slavery of Egypt) illustrates clearly the fickle nature of man to the love of God. The powerful attraction of Israel to the idols of the nations among whom they moved is a warning as to how easy it is for us to seek the idols and patterns of behaviour that characterize the culture in which we live.

If there is mutual agreement that the time is right for a pastoral change, and the process is entered into prayerfully with careful planning and mutual respect, the painful aspects of change can be coped with much more effectively. It is still essential that there be appropriate good-byes. The art of saying good-bye must be lovingly and humbly entered into if a God-honouring closure to one's ministry is to be accomplished. Leaving clean and completing resolution of relationships may often be accomplished with acceptable rituals and ceremonies of appreciation. Each community will have different processes of closure such as farewell banquets, opportunity for expressions of gratitude or other celebrations.

When a pastor leaves in anger, the result is often residual conflict. However, when good closure is accomplished, thanksgiving, gratitude, and celebration are coupled with hope and results in well-being. Both pastor and congregation can reflect on the gains, the growth, and the learning that has been achieved. This can lead to gratitude and praise to the Lord as His leading is experienced. Debriefing of the pastor and congregation, if done sensitively and with careful planning, can help toward a peaceful conclusion. It would be especially advantageous for denominational leadership to facilitate debriefing.

Whatever happened to motivate the severing of the relationship, leaving can have a large impact. There are two very important variables that are at the heart of one's experience of leaving. First, was it predictable? Secondly, was it voluntary? Leaving may not be purely one or the other but the degree to which these were involved will be very determinative of the experience of those involved. The following table (next page) identifies four Different Types of Transition from the perspective of the leaving being voluntary or predictable.

There may be varying degrees of each of these two factors. It is difficult to present concepts such as these in the reality of their dynamic interplay.

DIFFERENT TYPES OF TRANSITIONS

Type I Predictable & Voluntary	Type II Predictable & Involuntary
Type III Unpredictable & Voluntary	Type IV Unpredictable & Involuntary

Retirement may illustrate a Type I transition that is predictable and voluntary. For example, my retirement from full-time clinical and pastoral counselling was quite predictable after over fifty years of ministry. It was also voluntary and was strategically planned with the President of MHI. An element within that decision was finding a replacement and orchestrating a transition from my role as Director of Counselling Services to another person qualified and willing to assume that leadership.

Sometimes accidents or health issues may impact the timing of one's retirement. We may need the help of others to assist us in achieving objectivity so that we can make retirement a voluntary act. Frequently, loved ones or other caring individuals may be able to predict an opportune time for transition earlier than person in the situation. For this reason alone, it is important that others whom you trust be given the opportunity to share their insight and interact with you. The pain of leaving may be blinding and its many aspects do need to be prayerfully explored. This is often more effectively accomplished with objective input from sensitive people outside of the situation. Others whom we find trustworthy can be very helpful as they walk with us in discovering the will of God.

Each type of transition will differ according to the presence of these two variables. Transitions that are involuntary (i.e. Type II and IV) are frequently accompanied by pain from the trauma of fear of rejection, judgment, guilt, wrongful accusations or other reactive responses. The more unpredictable a transition, the less we are able to prepare for it through anticipatory planning. Trauma is frequently exacerbated by unpredictable transitions. When transition is necessitated by some dramatic event it is both involuntary and unpredictable, as is the case when civil war has occurred in countries where missionaries are serving. However, when *civil war* breaks out in a church, for whatever reason, the trauma and unrest generate tensions that sever relationships. Most pastors find conflict very difficult especially if they are compassionate and nurturing. Pastors who have endured unbearable situations experience depression, stress response, and self-incrimination. Such reactions create greatly magnified problems for the transition experience.

The real life stories of transition provided in chapter one illustrate these four different types of transition. Story one illustrates Type IV. The story of Philip illustrates the process whereby his transition became Type I through the affirmation of both his denomination and the church. It may be helpful for you to go back to the real life illustrations provided in that chapter to more fully grasp these different types of transition. Often, real life experience may be a mixture of types or will develop from one type to another if the opportunity for negotiation and interaction is provided. It is a great help to process and understand the *leaving* experience.

THE IN-BETWEEN STAGE

The time between ministries is *The In-Between Stage* of transition. It is at this point that one has left the shore and begun to cross over the river of transition. Sometimes, pastors leap into the swirling waters of transition and attempt to find their way across alone. Others enter the water accompanied by wife and family but otherwise make it a private experience. Often, it is the desire of the pastor and his spouse to protect their children from the pain of the experience, but this is often a two-edged sword. Children are very perceptive and, if not included in the process appropriately, will come to very immature decisions with dire consequences for themselves as well as their parents. One example of this was the total rejection of Christianity by children coupled with severe anger toward those whom they perceived to have abused their parents. The impact on children always requires serious consideration.

Personally, I would conclude that it is rarely appropriate for a pastor and spouse to try to cross this river alone. Individuality is a shaky craft and often does not survive the rapids and currents experienced in the crossing. We need the stability of a community where others can bring compassion, comfort, and objectivity. Frequently, the assistance of denominational leadership is crucial at this time, and professional counselling may bring an added dimension. In accepting the company and assistance of others the potential for a successful crossing is greatly enhanced.

This *In-Between stage* is for many people in ministry the most traumatic time, and it is different for everyone. The duress of the in-between stage has much to do with one's reasons for leaving and the effectiveness of the departure process. Regardless of the reason for leaving, being *In-Between* involves a loss of relationships, some degree of isolation, and loss of role, community, leadership, and belonging. It also brings self-defensiveness, anxiety, grief, stress response, and in every case some degree of anger. Whether one is able to identify these emotions, their related physiological and neurological response will be identifiable. Another strong element identified by pastors is an experience of *time without use*, which they feel is wasted. One pastor stated, "I feel so useless. I have all this time on my hands with nothing to do but wait." It is usually only a short time before pastors will complain about not knowing what to do with the time that previously had been occupied with ministry. It will be helpful to review the overview provided in the previous chapter to gain a broader perspective and sense that the *In-Between* stage does not go on forever.

Whether the decision to leave was motivated or initiated by the pastor, the people, a few people, the leadership of the church or the family of the pastor will be crucial. Of course, it will be different if the leaving was motivated by conflict, doctrinal issues, moral failure, a challenge of authority, or any number of other factors.

Let me emphasize that it is not only the pastor who needs consideration in a time of transition. The spouse, family (both immediate and extended), children, and of course the congregation and its leadership frequently need assistance to navigate these waters. Many of these will face loss, grief, anger, and numerous other emotions. The loss of friends, the need to move, and adjusting to a new community constitute the more trying aspects of transition. And people who have been deeply ministered to by the pastor may feel betrayed or abandoned when he leaves.

If the *In-Between* stage is of long duration, many more issues come to the fore. Financial stress will be great if there is no adequate severance. Moving may raise difficult issues concerning the education of children or switching of health care providers. Pastors who are between ministries must deal with spiritual issues such as identifying God's presence. Wives and children suffer greatly if they feel that the pastor has been rejected or perceived to have failed. One may feel like withdrawing from one's peers or on the other hand, may engage in defensive behaviour that exacerbates the problem and creates discomfort for peers.

There are a number of helpful ways to deal with these issues. Transition is a maze of turbulence that each person navigates uniquely. In the midst of this *in-between* stage, it is important to clarify many of the varied responses and mixed emotions we experience. Often the differences in our emotional responses become the focus of conflict. It is important that each be given a freedom for their own response and not pushed to deal with things in the same way as others. It may be helpful to review the discussion in chapter one where *the reflective pause* was discussed in detail. The reflective pause equates to finding a resting place, such as an island, in the midst of the river. It may be a sheltered cove such as Paul found when traversing the Mediterranean on his way to Rome. An island of respite in the midst of transition offers a place to explore each of these factors in quietness with the Lord.

The next two stages of transition will be discussed in a following chapter but before proceeding to that, it is essential to identify effective ways of dealing with issues related to loss of social posture, social status, and coping with our emotional responses. These will be organized around the theme of responding to transition in a manner that is facilitated by peace and quiet. Appropriate assistance will lead to accomplishment of desired outcomes. It is important to embrace the experience with a clear understanding so that necessary healing can take place. Healing is necessary whether the transition has been voluntary or involuntary. Whatever the experience has been, residual responses must be resolved, and they will be different for each person.

> Since you are precious and honoured in my sight,
>   and because I love you,
> I will give men in exchange for you and people in
>   exchange for your life.
> Do not be afraid, for I am with you.
>
> Isaiah 43:4

Questions for Reflection

What were your predominant feelings in the leaving and in-between stages? Do you identify with biblical characters such as Moses, Elijah, the three Hebrew youth in Daniel or with Job? Can you release the past into the hands of God and find a vision for the future? How well was the process of leaving handled by the church? Was there an acknowledgement of the various responses of members of the congregation? What major issues were acknowledged as being important to each member of your family?

Chapter Four

Responding to Transitions

> You're blessed when you've worked up a good appetite
> for God.
> He's food and drink in the best meal you'll ever eat.
>
> Beatitudes (MSG)

When navigating *The Leaving* and *The In-Between Stage* of transition, it is helpful to process these stages with someone who is able to bring objectivity from *outside* the situation, -someone who has the skills to encourage exploration toward new understanding. It is important that this assistant be equipped to examine these matters from a biblical and theological perspective with an adequate level of interpersonal skill in communication, problem solving, and reflective creativity. The following procedure can be provided by another pastor, a mentor or mature friend who is able to commit the time necessary to move toward healing.

Debriefing: A Reflective Pause

It is most effective in working with people in transition to follow a fairly well-researched and structured process of debriefing. Some of the issues to be addressed are experiences

Debriefing is Reflective Pause

of change, trauma, cross-cultural deployment, and vocational placement. In this book, debriefing will be approached in its application to people in ministry, broadly defined.

Debriefing may be described as a *reflective pause* for personal inventory. The intent is to reflectively examine one's transition so as to achieve learning or growth that the Spirit of God may wish to engender. A quiet, uninterrupted period of time dedicated to this purpose is essential. The physical environment should be such as to provide a comfortable, noise-free atmosphere. Exploration is best conducted when there is no pressure or necessity to come to an immediate conclusion or decision. The purpose early on is to be open to new perspectives, thoughts, and information. Openness to new ways of seeing things is essential. We are often anchored by our attraction to the status quo, which inhibits innovative thinking. Innovation has been described as the outcome of a new idea colliding with an old idea to create a new way of seeing things. It is necessary to resist our attraction to the status quo. We need to expose ourselves to the viewpoint of others. This is the purpose of the *reflective pause*. Choose with care someone who can walk with you through the experience who does not have a need for quick answers.

Experience has shown that there is a preferred path that leads to the best results. First, it is important to clarify the facts and collect information in a non-judgmental fashion. What were the behaviours that led to the transition experience? It is often difficult to achieve a clear picture that is not contaminated by personal feelings, interpretations, and the premature attribution of motives. Establishing the facts creates some distance between one's feelings and the actual events. You may recall the lead actor in *Dragnet* constantly reiterating, "Just the facts, Ma'am! Just the facts!" Separating

Chapter 4: Responding to Transitions

the facts from our feelings helps avoid anchoring ourselves in destabilizing emotions. Wrapping our identity in fluctuating feelings of rejection, loss, grief or anger leads only to despair.

Secondly, once that separation has been achieved, we can then examine the *original* feelings that were experienced in response to our transition. It is equally important to explore the feelings of others who were affected by the same event. For example, we may reflect on how our spouse, the leader, bystanders, or others understood and responded to the situation. Looking at the response of others broadens the pastor's perspective and assists in movement toward greater objectivity, plus it generates empathy for others and helps to avoid self-centeredness.

Thirdly, while it is important to understand one's emotions, one must also move on to look at what the experience meant to each person involved. And, it is important to distinguish between feelings and their underlying meaning. Each of us interprets our experiences with personal meaning. It is essential to understand that events have different meaning for every individual and the perspective of each person must be respected. One outcome of recognizing these differences is that it enables the individual to loosen their grip on the highly personalized meaning they have ascribed to the incident. Meaning can only be shared beneficially when differences are honoured. Differing perspectives will often contribute to a more creative analysis and conclusion. When we talk to others who see everything from the same perspective that we do, it is not much better than talking to oneself; we may simply be reinforcing our own limited view of events.

Fourthly, it is helpful to imagine God's perspective of the event. In counselling, I will often ask that we imagine Jesus standing by, observing the events as they took place. What would his responses have been? This imaginative process often helps clarify what God might wish us to learn from our experience. The requirement is that we open ourselves to be hospitable to the Spirit of God who can then bring new and different meaning to what we have experienced. A strong theology of the sovereignty of God and the work of the Holy Spirit, coupled with God's love, provides a firm foundation for such discussion.

The function of the mentor in this reflective process is to provide feedback and facilitate reflection. The guide must retain a calm, nonjudgmental, accepting attitude. He is not there to mitigate pain or pass judgment or to assess, but to facilitate inquiry and foster openness to the ministry of the Spirit of God. Though it is essential to understand the spiritual dimensions in debriefing, this is usually not the best place to start. It is important to understand that the facilitator is not providing direction or answers, but rather, providing the opportunity for the pastor to reflect on his experience from as many vantage points as possible. The facilitator is not simply an answering machine but rather a fellow traveller who comes alongside a brother to study the experience and open hearts together, so as to receive God's direction and nurture. To be clear, at this point in the process the pursuit is empathic support, achievement of understanding, and objectivity. Answers, decisions, and action will come later. The debriefing is intentional, guided, and focused and is to be entered into in an environment conducive to the desired outcome. This requires privacy, confidentiality, patience, prayer, and an attitude of openness for sensitive exploration. The guidance of the Spirit of God is essential.

Debriefing: A reflective pause

Reflection on
- Ministry
- Family: self, spouse, children, extended family
- Relationships with church: leadership, congregation
- Changes re: ministry development, and one's response
- Challenges, successes, stress, joys
- Physical well-being and ill-health

Refocusing through
- Clarifying goals
- Revising goals
- Understanding changing family needs
- Considering life cycle changes that may impact ministry

Rearranging of Priorities
- In response to growth in ministry skills or new gifts discovered
- In response to changing opportunities of ministry
- In response to changes in organizational priorities

Rest and Recuperation
- Assessing need for rest, recuperation, renewal – spiritual, physical, social
- Intentionally designing and mapping transition time
- Considering training opportunities or re-deployment opportunities

The diagram on the previous page is suggestive of what will be explored during the time of debriefing. It is assumed that the process will be conducted over a period of time, with space in between sessions for the individual to seek the guidance of the Holy Spirit.

It usually is necessary to meet over several sessions to work one's way through debriefing. We may view debriefing as an opportunity, through reflection, to achieve new self-awareness. Everyone has the ability to reflect on the past and to anticipate the future, and if we can open ourselves to do so, we can achieve new learning. This requires a purposed avoidance of defensiveness and the pursuit of authenticity and integrity.

Avoiding defensiveness is not easy. Paul makes an interesting observation when he speaks of self-judgment and the judgment of others: "I care very little if I am judged by you or any human court; indeed, I do not even judge myself. My conscience is clear, but that does not make me innocent."[16] We must be open to facing the reality that even though we have a clear conscience it does not mean we are innocent. On the other hand, it is important not to turn an experience of transition into a guilt trip. Following the above-mentioned comment, Paul indicates that clear and unambiguous judgment will only occur when the Lord comes. In this life we can see only partially. We must understand that neither we nor others have the wisdom or knowledge to adequately assess the mystery associated with ministry for God. Humility must guide our approach in hearing the judgment of others and in self-judgment.

We must guard against the self-pity that comes with failure to meet the expectation of others or ourselves. Objectivity

---

16   1 Corinthians 4:3-4

usually shows that the pastor was not the only person in the equation. There is a need for balance between taking all the blame and refusing to acknowledge personal responsibility. Looking at past experiences with frank honesty and realism can be the pathway to very effective learning. The kind of analysis that leads to paralysis can often be avoided with the help of a sensitive fellow traveller.

Acknowledging the pain associated with transition is important. The reality is that tragedy is often a better teacher than success. A healthy perspective will view past failure as an opportunity to learn what can change the future. It is an opportunity to retune, refocus, and renew one's commitment by re-framing one's experience from God's perspective. It may involve an act of faith to discover God's presence in the pain of transition. The reflective pause can give birth to celebration as we discover God's hand in things that did not turn out the way we expected or hoped they would.

Gaining a New Perspective

Let me illustrate. As a young person growing up in what was essentially a *survival society* (1930s and 1940s) all materials were used frugally. When a sweater wore through at the elbows, we unravelled the wool. Unravelling the sweater and balling the wool was a job given to my older brother and me. The recovered yarn was reknit into mittens or scarves, or another sweater. This seemed like a big and important task to us, as young boys.

Debriefing gives a person the opportunity to unravel their experience and reknit it with meaning and significance that may at first have escaped their understanding. There is no one-pattern solution; debriefing must be adapted to each individual. For maximum learning and growth to occur in breaking free from the past, debriefing is essential. The biblical test in Psalm 51:10-12 becomes the prayer of debriefing: "Create in me a pure heart, O God, and renew a steadfast spirit within me. Do not cast me from your presence or take your Holy Spirit from me. Restore to me the joy of your salvation and grant me a willing spirit, to sustain me."

There are biblical models of debriefing. Jesus debriefed his disciples on their return from ministry.[17] Of course, it would be helpful to have much more detail as to his discussion with them. One may consider his interaction in Peter's restoration as evidencing aspects of debriefing.[18] It is also instructive to study Moses's conversations with God and his intercession on behalf of the Israelite people,[19] which provides a model of debriefing. As with most biblical leaders, he was a reluctant responder to God's invitation but experienced a clear and persistent call from God who acknowledged his weaknesses and assured him that he could accomplish his purposes through him. This clearly placed Moses in a dependent relationship with God. His intimacy with God sustained him in the face of great obstacles. In Deuteronomy (31-33) his farewell speech and transference of ministry to Joshua provides a model that should characterize the conclusion of each pastor's ministry.

Conversations with God are an essential part of transition, especially during the In-Between Stage when one is assessing their ministry and projecting toward the future. Ideally, debriefing leads to conversation with God that is deep, personal and definitive in terms of ministry. God's conversation

---

17   Matthew 10; Mark 6:6ff; and Luke 10:1-20
18   John 21:15ff; See Chapter 2
19   See Exodus chapters 3, 32-34 and Numbers 14

with Elijah provides a helpful study when we are discouraged, weary, lonely or fearful in ministry. Elijah also provides an example of transference of his ministry over to Elisha.[20]

Other biblical examples offer glimpses; both Jesus and Paul spent significant time in the desert alone with God in preparation for ministry. Daniel and his partners transitioned from one culture to another with clearly defined commitment as to how they were going to function in their new situation.[21] Their resolve was not to defile themselves but to remain faithful. The principle illustrated here may be stated as follows: clarify your commitment before the test of circumstance. Joseph transitioned from one role to another during his time in Egypt. Jonah actually resisted transitioning from a ministry in which he was comfortable to an experience he did not want and to which he bitterly objected. He encountered major difficulty during his days of disobedience but in later obedience he also endured very stressful and disruptive emotions when God did not do what Jonah thought he should. He did not understand God's response to repentance and his willingness to let God be a God of grace was way off base. Jonah had a great opportunity to learn much about himself in God's debriefing of him though it remains unclear whether he took advantage of that opportunity.

Many pastors have found debriefing to be a cleansing time that affirmed their giftedness and brought greater focus to their ministry. Whenever transitions are entered into there are endings that must be cared for and dealt with in integrity, humility, and grace. Endings in one ministry may lead to beginnings that provide opportunities for re-focusing, re-tooling, renewing one's commitments, identifying new directions, and leaving old

---

20   2 Kings 2
21   Daniel 1:8

patterns to shape new ones. The crisis of transition becomes the opportunity to learn all that God wishes to teach us, whether through celebration or through suffering. God will lead us to new perspectives concerning ourselves and our potential for ministry if we open our hearts and minds to him. His faithfulness to his servants in Scripture attests to this.

Gaining a new perspective may involve seeing whatever tension or conflict there may have been in initiating the transition from a different perspective. Conflict is often discussed in terms of management and resolution. In reality, many conflicts are not manageable or resolvable. We must look beyond the conflict to learn and transform the experience of conflict through reframing or reknitting it into a faith perspective. In the end, we may discover that the ending was necessary for reasons only God can enable us to see through eyes of faith. The goal is to seek God's perspective and healing in the dimensions of our lives where that is needed.

Acknowledging the Stress of Transition

We are created to respond to stress. A famous Canadian doctor of the last century spoke of good stress and bad stress. Good stress is that which calls on the body to respond according to its capacity, enabling us to accomplish tasks and maintain health. Stress activates our emotional, chemical, and muscular systems and when it is normal or slightly beyond normal, the effect is to increase our endurance. When stress goes beyond what we are capable of handling, it creates wear and tear on the body. This is also the case when stress becomes chronic or recurs with greater frequency than we are able to handle. Wear and tear accumulates to where it becomes destructive, and symptoms manifest themselves wherever our physical or emotional system is weakest.

The symptoms of stress are to some degree peculiar to each person but the overall response is quite identifiable. Each person has a stress threshold beyond which stress begins to be harmful. The autonomic nervous system plays a central role in activating the body as do hormones, blood pressure, heart rate and other physiological responders to stress. We are physiologically and emotionally prepared to begin a *fight*, *flight* or *freeze* response to stress. These responses will manifest in every dimension of our being and relationships.

PERSONAL INDICATORS OF STRESS
(Glenn C. Taylor, 1991)

HEALTH INDICATORS
- __ fatigue & chronic exhaustion
- __ frequent & prolonged colds
- __ headaches (tension or migraine)
- __ sleep disturbances
    - -insomnia
    - -nightmares
    - -excessive sleeping
- __ gastro-intestinal disorders
- __ ulcers
- __ hypertension
- __ heart disease
- __ vague viral-like symptoms
- __ muscle or skeletal pain
- __ sudden loss or gain of weight
- __ flare-up of pre-existing problems
- __ increased premenstrual tension
- __ injuries from high risk behaviour
- __ excessive sweating or urination

BEHAVIOUR INDICATORS
___ nervous behaviour
___ extreme mood or behavioural changes
___ increase use of addictive substances
___ high risk-taking behaviour
___ hyperactivity
___ change in sexual behaviour or dysfunction
___ withdrawal from activity
___ over or under eating

EMOTIONAL ADJUSTMENT INDICATORS
___ emotional distancing
___ paranoia
___ depression, sadness, discouragement
___ smoldering resentment
___ decreased emotional control
___ martyrdom
___ fear of going crazy
___ increased amount of daydreaming/fantasy
___ constant sense of being 'trapped'
___ undefined fears
___ inability to concentrate
___ regression

RELATIONSHIP INDICATORS
___ isolation from, or over-bonding with others
___ general critical attitude
___ irritability, impatience, hatred
___ rebellion against authority
___ immoral behaviour
___ increased marital or family conflict
___ increased interpersonal conflict
___ reversals of usual behaviour
___ mistrust of friends or family
___ inability to make decision
___ forgetfulness of appointments, deadlines, etc.

ATTITUDE INDICATORS

__ self-condemnation
__ sense of total inadequacy
__ frequent spells of brooding
__ boredom
__ sick sense of humor
__ tragic sense of life attitude
__ attitudes of self-righteousness
__ hypercritical of organizations or peers
__ demonstrations of despair
__ expressions of false guilt
__ overwhelming sense of loss or grief

SPIRITUAL VALUE INDICATORS

__ loss of faith
__ spiritual crisis
__ sudden & extreme changes in values or beliefs
__ loss of hope or loss of anticipation
__ blaming God
__ spiritualizing of problems that may be physical, emotional, or medical
__ withdrawal from, or critical of one's faith community
__ movement to legalism, rigidity, critical attitude
__ movement into 'cults' or submissiveness or denial of responsibility for self

The above instrument is one that I use with pastors who have experienced significant stress. Many pastors who completed this exercise quickly began to understand the impact of stress upon their lives. It is often very helpful to consult with one's spouse or a close friend who may assist in identifying where stress manifests itself. The body, soul, and mind of man continuously seek a state of homeostasis that when disrupted by excessive stress, leads to a chronic state. For those who are not aware of the presence of stress it is necessary to rely on evidence that can be identified in the chart above or on feedback

Grief in Transitions

Another helpful perspective from which to view transition has to do with the dimension of loss involved. Transition always involves loss. The losses experienced when a ministry is terminated are real regardless of the reason for the termination. An understanding of grief will enlighten our perspective of transition. The terminating of one's ministry leads to a loss of relationships with many individuals and the accompanying familiarity of comfortable habits. Often there is a loss of friendships for all members of the family and a breaking of relationships with persons to whom one has ministered to at a level of deep bonding. There will normally be a change of home relationships, community relationships, and relationships with others who remain engaged in ministry.

Grief literature usually lists five stages of grieving: denial (which may lead to shock or escape), anger (expressed to experience emotional release, depression, anxiety, panic), bargaining (usually attempting to negotiate with others or God), Guilt (attributing blame to self, recrimination for failure, feeling abandoned), and acceptance or adaptation (rallying resources to seek a new future). Most of the literature acknowledges that in grief there is protest, despair, and detachment. These appear to be universal regardless of age although they are neither rigid nor the same for each individual. However, emotional upheaval, anger, self-doubt, depression, and anxiety are also almost always present.

The Bible contains examples, of which Job is a classic. The blackness and bleakness with which he responded to his experience of loss is unrestrained. He manifests all of the symptoms that accompany grief: sadness, desire for death, helplessness, sleep disturbance, a sense of the worthlessness of life, pessimism, and many different physical manifestations of stress. If you have ever driven through intense fog on a highway or on the water, you will understand that wandering in grief is much like that. It is helpful to examine the imagery with which Job defines his grief. "Now that God has unstrung my bow and afflicted me, they throw off restraint in my presence. On my right the tribe attacks; they lay snares for my feet, they build their siege ramps against me…Terrors overwhelm me; my dignity is driven away as by the wind, my safety vanishes like a cloud. And now my life ebbs away; days of suffering grip me. Night pierces my bones; my gnawing pains never rest."[22] Note the despair, the loss of effectiveness, the sense of abandonment, the physical pain, the anxiety, and the sleep deprivation. Job feels completely abandoned by God and friends.

Grief will be one of most significant issues to address in the process of debriefing during *The In-Between Stage* of transition. Frequently, pastors who leave churches on friendly terms to pursue a call to new ministry do not adequately deal with the losses entailed in transition. The consequences of burying grief can be confusing and debilitating—like a festering sore that goes untreated. Appropriate grieving frees one to move into the future.

---

22   Job 30:11-17

Critical Incident Stress Debriefing

Debriefing and healing from grief, as indicated, may be guided by a peer, a coach, a mentor, or a spiritual guide. However, when there has been excessive pain or trauma associated with the departure from a ministry it may be necessary to seek professional help. Professionally trained intervention would be indicated in the presence of overt medical, psychiatric or psychological issues in a venue that includes professional expertise. Some leavings are sufficiently traumatic as to require therapeutic intervention. In the real life illustrations provided earlier in chapter one, George, Sam, and Eric are examples where therapeutic intervention would greatly facilitate their leaving the past behind so they might move into the future. This is not to advocate that all receive such help, but to encourage openness to explore the level of assistance needed as determined by the symptoms present.

In the last two decades of twentieth century, mental health professionals began to look more closely at how people respond to crisis. Traumas are now referred to as *critical incidents*. People respond to traumatic events with rather specific responses. Critical incidents may be situations that are life threatening and emotionally disturbing or they may be personally distressing experiences arising from unexpected events, accidents, death of others or very traumatic change that has a most pervasive effect. People are affected cognitively (inability to concentrate, self-blame, repetitive thought patterns), emotionally (shock, vulnerability, loss of emotional control), physiologically (fatigue, nightmares, startle response), behaviourally (avoidance, alienation, substance abuse), and spiritually (loss of faith, hopelessness, anxiety, anger toward God). When a number of these symptoms are present, professional help is usually indicated. This intervention is called Critical Incident Stress Debriefing (CISD).

CISD is a more highly structured form of debriefing. It will be most effective with pastors if the ending was of a traumatic nature and led to the intrusive symptoms indicated above. In such cases the pastor should be referred to a professional who can assess the need and guide the process. It is of great importance for other pastors, mentors or theologically trained persons to be part of the ongoing assistance. Most professionals would welcome that involvement. Christian friends should not abandon a fellow-believer at this time.

Let me reiterate; firstly, when a pastor is experiencing transition he will almost invariably need and benefit from a debriefing experience. Secondly, it is important to view the transition experience from the perspective of dealing with grief. Thirdly, it is necessary to acknowledge transition with a view to the degree of stress experienced. Fourthly, if there is evidence of trauma it is extremely important for this to be promptly assessed by someone trained in CISD. Urgency is indicated because CISD is most effective if entered into within three days of the evidence of symptoms. Fifthly, it is important that the pastor be open to exploring the range of his responses to transition and be willing to access the assistance he needs with someone who is skilled and compassionate. Another avenue of healing that has been quite effective involves debriefing in a small group of peers. In this situation it is important to have within the group the gifted personnel necessary to guide things in a productive direction. On the other hand, the situation may require medical or professional counselling to address issues that require expertise commensurate with manifest needs.

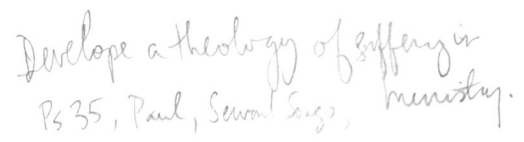

DEALING WITH THE RESPONSE OF OTHERS

The public nature of transition means that many people will have only partial knowledge. The complexity of many situations makes it difficult to know what to share or how widely information should be disclosed. Each situation must deal with a variety of responses, some of which may add to the hurt and the confusion.

The question of how to deal with the judgment of others and one's own hypercritical self-judgment during transition is almost always a factor. Personality variables play a large role in determining how we deal with criticism both in the expression of and our response to any critique. Of course, the source of the criticism will be of primary concern. The wise person will receive the judgment of others, weigh it carefully, and determine what is actually applicable or what arises simply out of misinformation or misunderstanding. But the reactive person will respond with defensiveness, anger or the deflection of criticism back onto others. The Scriptures provide abundant evidence that ministry elicits opposition. However, we also elicit opposition by immature, aggressive, or inappropriate leadership styles. When we look at conflict, the usual conclusion is that both parties have contributed. Each person must examine his own heart before God with as much openness and honesty as possible in assessing their personal contribution and that of others.

Paul experienced many transitions in his ministry as well as much conflict and criticism. In this vein, it would be well to develop a theology of suffering in ministry. One might begin such a study by exploring the Servant passages in Isaiah and other servants of God who had to cope with criticism. Paul received considerable criticism from people in Corinth, and with it there was much tension in the church there.

> So then, men ought to regard us as servants of Christ and as those entrusted with the secrets of God. Now it is required that those who have been given a trust must prove faithful. I care very little if I am judged by you or by any human court; indeed, I do not even judge myself. My conscience is clear, but that does not make me innocent. It is the Lord who judges me. Therefore judge nothing before the appointed time; wait till the Lord comes. He will bring to light what is hidden in darkness and will expose the motives of men's hearts. At that time each will receive his praise from God.[23]

In this brief passage much is relevant to our discussion. Those engaged in ministering are "servants of Christ." The reality is that the relationship between a pastor and a church is not simply an employer-employee relationship. One's calling by God as a servant of Christ is the first priority. The servant functions as one executing a *sacred trust* and must first be found faithful to this trust. Human judgment must take a back seat to this very foundational reality. Each pastor must understand what that sacred trust entails and how it impacts his life. It does not free him from the covenantal role he enters into with a church but is foundational to pastor-church relationships. The covenant relationship between a pastor and a church involves a solemn commitment and one that must be balanced with the personal calling of God and an all-important interplay with other leaders in the church. Added to that is the responsibility for community among churches in a given denomination and the relationship between the church and the larger social community in which it exists.

---

23   1 Corinthians 4:1-5

There is interdependency between all of these levels of relationship and authority.

Paul sought the wisdom of the Jerusalem counsel and encouraged the responsibility of churches for one another. This principle must be given the weight it deserves. The relationship of the "servant of Christ" to those he serves and to other servants of Christ is important. The interplay between Christ, the pastor, church leadership, the church, and the social community needs to be understood. For example, Christ informed Peter that John was Christ's servant and not the responsibility of Peter.[24] Peter was to focus on *his* specific calling. There will almost always be distinctiveness in our ministry and a personal trust that is ours alone to fulfill. Great caution must be exercised in comparing our calling to the ministry of others who are equally personally responsible to Christ.

An important aspect of self-understanding for every pastor is to understand his personal response to criticism and differences of opinion. If a reactive response is your default position, that should be addressed. If your default is submissiveness or retreat, that should be examined. Early in my counselling career I sought the help of a supervisor. It was rather easy for me to be gentle, kind, and loving in relationships when providing care for people. However, when confrontation was necessary, I would back away. The phrase my supervisor drilled into my head week by week was, "Taylor, don't be nice, be helpful!" The balance between assertiveness and gentleness is not an easy one to achieve.

The humility we need to be a servant of others requires from us a repentant heart that is open to whatever nurturing correction we might receive from the Lord and from fellow believers. If a pastor is unable to see himself as part of the

---

24   John 21:21-23

problem he will not likely go on to be part of the solution. The Lord knows our hearts even if we don't, but only an open heart will receive the Spirit's guidance in the introspective process of becoming more effective in ministry. Debriefing, processing grief, acknowledging the role of stress and receiving objective input from others can be immensely helpful in achieving the balance we need.

Acquiring an understanding of why this transition has occurred must include acknowledging the contribution of many factors and especially those that the pastor himself brings to the termination of his ministry. Some pastors are bullies and are very aggressive in their leadership style. This generates conflict and leads to people being hurt. Passive pastors fail to lead and foster the opportunity for the emergence of other leaders who may lead from inappropriate motives. And there are many pastors who experience moral failure. Sometimes this occurs as an outcome of over-extension or unwise involvement in ministry to hurting people. Then, some church leaders function out of a stance of power and influence so as to control others, perhaps through financial contributions in exchange for dominance. Openness to explore all possibilities frequently leads to sufficient understanding for one to move forward in ministry. However, we must acknowledge the complexity of these situations and carefully seek the guidance and wisdom that God alone can provide. One must tread slowly in the midst of such a maze of human entanglement.

The dynamics of ministry retain mystery; there is so much that is hidden and known only to the mind of God. Jesus talked to Nicodemus[25] about spiritual birth as being a work of God's Spirit and the life flowing therefrom, like the mystery of the wind. All that goes on in ministry has myste-

---

25 John 3:1-21

rious elements whether one thinks of God's call to ministry or the fruit of that ministry in the lives of others. We remain very much dependent upon this mysterious working of God; this is especially the case for the pastor in his journey in ministry. The ebb and flow of ministry must be envisioned through eyes of faith in an ever-unfolding exploration of faith, seeking and submitting to his shepherding ways by the help of the Holy Spirit. Humility in ministry requires an open heart as we move along the pathway of ministry. We must come to rest in the comfort of his love and grace. It is in this context of divine nurturing that adjustments are made to our self-awareness and self-definition. The transition periods of our lives are God's provision of the opportunity for us to break the bonds of the past and enter into newness of life and renewed ministry.

Hezekiah said,

> I will walk humbly all my years because of this anguish of my soul.
> Lord, by such things men live; and my spirit finds life in them too.
> You restored me to health and let me live.
>
> Isaiah 38:15-16

QUESTIONS FOR REFLECTION

Am I willing to invest in a *reflective pause* facilitated by someone capable of providing the spiritual leadership needed? Have I worked through the grief related to my losses, both personal and otherwise? Am I being too critical of myself, too closed to the critique of others and insufficiently open to the Spirit of God in assessing my role and that of others?

What are the possible learning achievements that I can take with me into the future? How can I re-knit the past to create a more effective ministry in the future?

Chapter Five

Facing the Prospects of a New Ministry

> You're blessed when you care.
> At the moment of being *care-full* you will find yourself cared for.
>
> Beatitudes (MSG)

The next few chapters will explore stages four and five of the transition process. God's call to ministry is a high and holy calling; however, in the midst of transition many question their calling. As I mentioned earlier, statistics indicate that a very large number of pastors leave the ministry when in the midst of transition. Transition *out* of ministry is sometimes more bearable than a transition *into* ministry if leaving the previous ministry was painful. No one wants to experience the pain associated with transition a second or third time if the transition has been initiated by problems or conflict. Previous chapters have provided some suggestion for dealing with transition. Having experienced a *reflective pause* in the midst of the river of transition, we must now land on the other shore and begin setting up camp. If we have adequately processed the *Leaving* and the *In-Between stage* in crossing the river, we will be anxious to begin a new ministry, that is, to set up camp in a new opportunity of service.

Leaving the Past and Moving Forward

When preparing to step ashore, having crossed the river, we need to step onto the new shore with a clear confidence in a sovereign God. Hope must be re-awakened by faith resting upon the love of God. Jesus assured his disciples that when they reached the other side of their pain in losing him, the Comforter would come to lead them into new adventures of ministry. It was only by looking back that they would understand what his teaching, death, and resurrection really meant. He assured them that after their experience of anxiety, confusion, and grief, they would understand and receive the gift of the Spirit who would enable them to fulfill his work in the world.

Before moving ahead we do well to learn from the past. Peterson, in The Message, entitles Isaiah 43: "When You're Between a Rock and a Hard Place." Isaiah's encouraging message in verses 16-21 could be summarized with these few words:

> This is what God says…Forget about what's happened; don't keep going over old history. Be alert, be present. I'm about to do something brand new. It's bursting out! Don't you see it? There it is! I'm making a road through the desert, rivers in the badlands… Drinking water for my chosen people, the people I made especially for myself …[26]

The prophet excitedly anticipates the deliverance of God for his chosen people.

---

26 Zondervan, *Parallel Study Bible*, (Grand Rapids, MI.: Zondervan, 2008) Isaiah 43 (MSG)

Chapter 5: Facing the Prospects of a New Ministry

Forgetting the past is not easy. Frequently, the unfinished business of the past clings to us like barnacles to a ship. Boats need to be lifted into dry dock to have their hulls cleaned; pastors need to intentionally engage a process to experience the soul-cleansing that is part of leaving the past in order to create a new future. This is why understanding the experience of transition and entering into the processes outlined in the previous chapter are so important. The heart issue involved with freeing oneself from the tyranny and pain of the past is forgiveness. Forgiveness is the antidote to accumulated bitterness and resentment toward experiences of the past. When we have drained the cup of the past of all it can teach us, we must empty the dregs that remain by committing the rest to God's sovereign justice. We must set God above it all and dwell in him in grace, forgiveness, and peace.

Pain is a measurable biological phenomenon impacting our nervous system and brain chemistry in a way that has serious cognitive ramifications. Pain is also experienced at a deep emotional level and is perceived as suffering. Many pastors will associate aspects of transition with suffering. Some will acknowledge their contribution to a forced transition. Others see themselves as innocent victims of the sinful behaviour of others. If guilty, one must confess, repent, and seek forgiveness both from those we offended and from God. If innocent, we are not obliged to continue as a victim but can free ourselves through forgiving the wrongdoer and seeking refuge in the love of God. Retention of resentment, neurotic guilt, or anger causes one to nurture oneself on the toxins of another's behaviour. Paul speaks of the mystery of entering into Christ's sufferings, which may be a consequence of ministry on Christ's behalf.

We need the faith to believe that God can take us through the waters of a transition and into the future of his purpose for us. I associate this faith with what Paul expressed so aptly: "Forgetting what is behind and straining toward what is ahead, I press toward the goal to win the prize for which God has called me heavenward in Christ Jesus."[27] In as much as we have been called of God, it is helpful to remind ourselves of Paul's affirmation of Timothy, Titus, and all his other fellow workers, recognizing that we, like them, are called to a holy life of endurance.[28] To use different imagery, when racing a sailboat you do not attain speed if you are dragging an anchor. The anchor must either be dropped and left behind or taken on board and stowed in its rightful place. Accordingly, we dare not drag encumbering baggage from the past into our future. Having learned all we can, we must move on. We must not become entangled as Job's friends who could see no further than their immediate rationalizations (which took them far from God's perspective). When we wish to lay blame, we would do well to remember the response of Jesus to the disciples' question, "Who sinned, this man or his parents?" Jesus responded, "Neither...but this happened so that the work of God might be displayed."[29] Can we believe that what happens to us is related to God at work in our lives?

As important as it is to forget the past and seize the future, it is equally important to remember the lessons of the past. The Scripture is emphatic about our need to remember the faithfulness and deliverance of God in the past. Forgetting God's prior redeeming acts of intervention robs us of our greatest resource for walking by faith. The memory is by nature selective but as we move forward we must fill our minds

---

27 Philippians 3:13-14
28 See 1 Timothy 6:11; 2 Timothy 1:9; 2:24; 3:17; 4:5
29 John 9:1-5

with those experiences of God that nurture our confidence in his goodness and provision.

Anticipating a New Beginning

There are helpful things to do as one prepares to step ashore from the journey across the river of transition. Debarking from the boat and taking with you a reframed experience of the past starts a new beginning. First, one faces the invigorating challenge of change. Secondly, it is helpful to differentiate between generalized vocational call and the call to participate in a specific ministry.[30] Adjusting to and understanding these two important considerations will help us achieve a sense of freedom when embarking on a new ministry. Thirdly, this is a wonderful opportunity to rethink one's ministry in new and different ways.

As stated earlier, a clean break with the past, coupled with a celebratory remembrance of God's grace helps to create a renewed vision of the potential of God's grace in your future. Entering a new ministry requires a fresh beginning unencumbered by trash from the past. Moving from the past to the future is not traversed well if the path is cluttered with litter from previous encounters. Crossing the river of transition must take us through the turbulent waters of the present and beyond past experiences. Resolving issues of the past frees us for a new future. Sometimes, restoration of relationships from the past is a possibility, but if that is not possible, there must at least be restoration in our own heart and mind through forgiveness and grace. We must not drag the past along with us into the future. Where a complete resolution of the past is not possible, we must leave the past with God and commend

---

30 This is clarified later in this chapter.

it to him to deal with in his wisdom and grace. It is important to move forward with peace of mind and heart so that we may enter the future with the zeal for God that ministry requires.

THE CHALLENGE OF CHANGE

Transition is all about change. It is about endings and new beginnings and opportunity for change. Change challenges our status quo—our state of homeostasis, stability, and comfort. It is normal to resist change. There is comfort in the security of having a place to be, even if that place has become a rut. Ruts are comfortable but rarely fulfill our expectations. Ruts are comfortable because we can move along in them without much thought. When this happens, we remain in the *default* position. The default position is the safe place we fall back to when unsure of how to respond to a new stressor. It may not lead us where want to go, but being a reflex response, it feels comfortable.

Sometimes it takes great effort to get out of our ruts whether in thinking or behaviour. We need to constantly challenge ourselves with new possibilities. I find it helpful to read widely of others who do things very differently and hold beliefs different than mine. I am challenged to review my own cherished patterns of behaviour and thinking. Reading only those authors and speaking with only those who espouse my own position is not much better than talking to myself, which only confirms my biases but takes me no further. A challenge that enables me to go exploring and possibly go beyond my own borders is helpful. Change ushers us into the necessary process of adaptation, inducing self-assessment. It also generates anxiety and the shock that accompanies the loss of a fulfilling ministry. Transition may be the jolt that frees us from our rut. People in transition must face this jolt with openness and honesty.

However, change may also be anticipated with curiosity, fear or distrust. When that occurs, we experience anticipatory anxiety. Such anxiety is crippling and creates heightened fear. Change coupled with fear and the resulting anticipatory anxiety often leads to depression and reduced ability in decision-making.

Even if leaving one ministry for another has the full consent of both church and pastor, there are still real anxieties to be faced. At times, the pressures of leaving may be masked by appropriate celebration. Some resist celebration but in most cases celebration is an excellent way to honour God's grace in the ministry that is concluding. Even if the leaving is a difficult one, it may still be appropriate to create an opportunity for those who wish to celebrate the concluding ministry to do so. Some may wish to celebrate one's ministry while others may not wish to be involved. If this reality is faced openly and people's choice is respected it is wise to proceed with those who wish to do so. The anger that may be present in some should not curtail the celebration of others.

On the other hand, it is not appropriate to spiritualize transition if that leads to covering up the pain or the problems associated with it. Fear and anxiety may be masked by bravado, but whatever our defence, anxiety will work its toxins into our system. The chemical changes in one's body, in response to the anxiety of change, act as accelerators. The psycho-physiological impact of anxiety is relentless and destructive even if we deny it. Inner turmoil does not dissipate when ignored or buried. The healthy response is to acknowledge and deal with the realities. Honouring emotions associated with change and providing for their expression in honesty and dignity is best.

My engagement with people in painful transitions led me to write the following in response to their experience.

People in Pain

Deep flowing pain
Cuts deeply in the soil of the soul
Eroding the top soil
Leaving barren rock,
Hard, impervious.

Emotions—sensitivity washed away
By sorrow, resentment, grief.
Hardness remains
Accompanied by aloneness,
Wrapped in cold misery.

Sometimes that river of pain
Flows underground
Removing foundation soil
Creating a hollow hole,
Washing the roots of life
Clean of nourishment
To shrivel and die.
The tree stands shortly
Only to topple and decay
For lack of rootedness.

Circled by chaos
The surge of sorrow
Rushes in shooting arrows,
Defenseless, I stand
Absorbing the pain
Swallowing sorrow
Choking on grief.

The challenge of change must be addressed. Each person will experience it in different ways. What stresses one person may not have the same effect on another. If we do not deal with pain, it will go underground and work in ways that undermine and damage future opportunities.

The spouse of a pastor may often bear the brunt of the challenge of change when transition occurs in ministry. It is essential to address any related issues faced by his wife and other family members. Deep fissures in families can result from overlooking family members. Love issues in protectiveness. When one family member experiences change or trauma it creates great pain for those who care. Experience has convinced me that the total family must be included in responding to transition. The most common response is for the focus of the spouse to be upon the pastor. Certainly, this is an appropriate response of love and concern and will contribute to the pastor's coping.

However, it is also helpful if the spouse can look at the processes of transition from a very personal perspective and recognize her experience and responses with specificity. I would encourage spouses to work through the issues identified very specifically in reference to their own experience, not just that of the person in the role of pastor. Similarly, children deserve our attention to honour their experience of the implication of a pastor experiencing transition. We must add to that the necessity of healing for the family as a unit. Each individual's experience is different. At the same time, the corporate impact on the family must receive due attention.

Facing Stressors with Help

It is difficult to face one's stressors, fears, anxieties, and insecurities alone. It is generally acknowledged that men are reluctant to share their emotional struggles. Let me confess that I fit that category! There is a tendency to internalize things in assumed confidence or conviction that men should be able to cope and pray things through with God's help.

Let me illustrate. After almost eight years engaged in an executive role in one of the most fulfilling ministry experiences for me, I felt clearly called to leave. This was a very challenging decision. My inclination was to make the break quick and clean, with my wife and God as the only participants in the decision. In a saner moment, I prayerfully sought God to give me a mentor who would pray with me both in timing my departure and in seeking a new ministry choice. There were several options to consider, but above all I needed a man of God with wisdom and a man of prayer. I was surprised when God directed me to a man who had considerable investment in two of the options under consideration for the future. However, would he influence me in *his* preferred direction? With considerable anxiety, I contacted him to arrange a meeting. I shared up front my fears and anxiety about his potential to influence my decision. However, I knew he was a man of prayer and wisdom. Clarification and direction was found through his sensitive and spiritual guidance, and a decision was reached. The following years convinced me that God had proved faithful. I felt like Moses when others held up his arms in support while he prayed.[31] The leaving was not easy but a new vision for future ministry was forged and proved God's faithfulness.

A great danger in transition is the avoidance of the anxiety associated with it. When we fail to embrace anxiety and deal with it openly, it becomes subversive. It will then manifest itself in secondary symptoms that are physical, emotional, relational or spiritual. Subversive symptoms inhibit progress. If you did

---

31 Exodus 17:8-16

not complete the instrument, *Personal Indicators of Stress*, in the previous chapter, let me suggest you do so at this point.

Another great danger is to turn to others for pity, that is, to seek reinforcement or sympathy for our plight. Sometimes sympathizing people are not the most helpful. It is common for people in the midst of such change to feel abandoned; we may seek the comfort of sympathy when that is not what is needed. Friends often do not know what to say and when they say nothing, the person experiencing change may feel even more alone or misunderstood. Yet saying too much, they replicate the experience of Job. Job's counselors were most effective in their seven days of silence. Their rationalizations when they began to talk simply increased Job's pain to the point where he cried: "How long will you torment me and crush me with words."[32] One's choice of counsel in dealing with stress and envisioning a new ministry is crucial.

Remember Sam, from chapter one.[33] He dropped out in discouragement and found himself without the support of those he had previously called his fellow workers. No one contacted him. He felt abandoned by his fellows and by God who, from his perspective, had failed to rescue him. He lapsed into depression as he buried his anger toward the system and toward the God who did not rescue him. He continued in that state for over twenty years.

The anxiety of change does not always lead to such an extreme response but failure to address it leaves deep and ugly scars. These, in turn generate a cynicism toward others and toward ministry. When the financial pressure of unemployment becomes an issue, anxiety is greatly increased. Worry about sustaining one's spouse and family become central issues.

---

32 Job 19:2
33 Chapter one, example three.

We can curse the pain of the past or design the future we desire. If we become locked in the pain, we will become critical of all who participated in the decisions that generated our pain. Anxiety, anger, hurt, loss or other emotions are dealt with more effectively if openly acknowledged. This is more likely to occur with some objective help. Paul wrote, "Carry each other's burdens, and in this way you will fulfill the law of Christ."[34] When Paul was *harassed at every turn – conflicts on the outside and fears within* and experiencing no rest in his body, he was comforted by God through the coming of his co-worker Titus.[35] This required openness on the part of Paul to be ministered to by Titus. It is important that we bring humility and receptivity when being ministered to by others. Their support can free us to experience much needed grace and to be appropriately forgiving toward those who may have contributed to our pain. In so doing, we free ourselves from the tyranny of our bad experience and the rejection we feel. If this happens we may discover that tragedy and pain are better teachers than success. Real and lasting growth is often the outcome of transition.

Vocational Call and Church Call

Clarifying the relationship of pastor and congregation may help in understanding transition. Ministry involves more than a contract between the pastor and the organization. There is a difference between a pastor's call from God to vocational ministry and the call of a church to him to participate in its ministry. Vocational call rests in a broader category and may express itself

---

34 Galatians 6:2
35 2 Corinthians 6:5-7

in many different types of ministry. Paul was very clear about his calling when he wrote to the churches of Galatia: "Paul, an apostle—sent not from men nor by man, but by Jesus Christ and God the Father"[36] Often, this distinction is unclear in both the mind of the pastor and the understanding of the church. It is helpful to see the distinction between the two.

In our consideration of transition, it is important not to confuse the rejection of one's ministry by a church or organization as rejection by God. Frequently, in counselling a pastor it becomes obvious that the termination has had much more to do with politics, competition for influence, leadership or personal preference than with the call of God. Many pastors suffer serious anxiety about their vocational call when they are rejected by a church or when the nurture of their friends or denomination is withdrawn.

Also, a pastor's sense of mission and calling is greatly enhanced by his perception of the relationship between his vocational call and how he perceives his giftedness. A scriptural study of spiritual gifting, and the sovereignty of God who distributes those gifts, led me to the conclusion that there is a tight correlation between giftedness and ministry. Vocational call is closely related to the gifts of grace manifested in a person's life. Spiritual giftedness may be confirmed by ordination through processes peculiar to each denomination. The input and affirmation of fellow pastors and the church community is a vital consideration. Not every ministry will present the opportunity to express all of the gifts of the individual. Thus, it becomes essential to discern how well a pastor's vocational call correlates with the opportunities of a specific situation. Avoidable tension arises when a congregation is not clear about this distinction.

---

36   Galatians 1:1

The other side of the coin must also be addressed. Whatever difference exists between the expectations of the pastor and those of the congregation is a fairly good predictor of future tension or conflict. The church is calling the pastor to fulfill a certain role within their congregation, and in this sense, they are the employer. However, it is not appropriate to think of the relationship simply in terms of an employer-employee relationship. The call of God and the call of the church must be kept in balance. It is helpful to ask pastors, "Did you come to this church with the intention of adapting to their culture and expectations, or did you expect them to adjust to you?" The same question could be asked of a church. Churches bring expectations that often reflect their history and relationship patterns with previous pastors. Churches that have a history of brief pastorates, tensions with previous pastors, financial shortfalls, tensions between elders and pastors, or a bad reputation in their community are likely to continue in that pattern. Pastors also bring their own history with them and often replicate their personal scenario from pastorate to pastorate. Unexamined history tends to repeat itself in destructive ways. It requires great sensitivity to assess the past of both church and pastor, but it must be done; otherwise trouble waits at the door.[37]

Debriefing during a time of transition can save much grief and open new possibilities for the future by providing an opportunity to clarify one's calling. It is necessary in the negotiations with the search committee for both pastor and church to explore such issues toward achieving mutual understanding. In this way all have a chance to acknowledge the past with humility and agree to create the future God wants

---

37 The selection process is outlined in Lance C. Johnson, *Pastor Search 411*, (Brampton, ON, Kainos, 2010)

for both. Without such openness and commitment, healthy change is unlikely to occur.

Recently the term *intentional interim pastor* has been used to define a role that is quite different from the role of an interim pastor. Such a person, specifically trained and invited for the purpose of addressing issues related to previous pastoral experience, may help a church to move beyond its past. Training opportunities for such ministry are currently available in some denominations.[38] This intentional ministry for a church has the potential to be just as beneficial as would be debriefing for a pastor. These two approaches may enable both church and pastor to leave the past behind and move to new expressions of ministry with more mutual cooperation. Effectiveness in ministry improves by learning from past experiences and intentionally creating the future one believes God wants.

Conclusion

It is helpful to think of transitions in ministry as phases or stages, and the change point as an opportunity for re-evaluation, clarification, and a new beginning. Many of the biblical models of ministry illustrate the need for knowing God and his specific will for his people as they responded to his call. Moses, Gideon, Isaiah, and Jeremiah were all reluctant to become leaders. They needed to know God, his specific calling and his equipping of them.

---

38 The Fellowship of Evangelical Baptists in Canada offered such training in the summer of 2012. They can be contacted for further information. Outreach Canada is one organization in this country that offers training for pastors who desire to assist churches in processing their experience of transition from one pastor to another. Find information on their web site, www.outreachcanada.org

Times of transition are occasions for us to seek God just as they did. Paul illustrates for us the difference between functioning as an evangelist in his first missionary journey and functioning in more pastoral ways as churches became established. Peter needed special intervention from God to understand how he was to minister to Gentiles as well as his own community. Jesus functioned differently when he was in Jerusalem, Samaria or Galilee. The opportunity to change ministries may be a gift of grace in which we retool and refocus to meet God in new challenges. A much needed *reflective pause* may create the space for God to do pruning that will increase our productivity for his kingdom. In his gentleness and grace, we become more fruitful. Readiness to create a new future is very dependent upon having effectively learned from the past and letting it go so that we are free to create a changed future.

In the next chapter we will identify other contributors to finding our place in ministry and understanding God's equipping us for his will.

> O Lord, be gracious to us; we long for you.
> Be our strength every morning, our salvation in times of distress…
> He will be the sure foundation for your times, a rich store of salvation
> and wisdom and knowledge; the fear of the Lord is the key to this treasure.
>
> Isaiah 32:2, 5-6

QUESTIONS FOR REFLECTION

What achievements in learning can you take with you to a new ministry? Are you dragging residual pain that should be dealt with? Do you characteristically go it alone or seek assistance in understanding your past and your future? Do you have difficulty accepting helpful rather than *nice* input from others? Can you clearly define how you would shape your future ministry differently? Can you release the past into the hands of God and find a vision for the future?

Chapter Six

Finding One's Place in Ministry

> You're blessed when you're content with just who you are – no more, no less.
> That's the moment you find yourself proud owners of everything that can't be bought."
> You're blessed when you get your inside world – your mind and heart – put right.
> Then you can see God in the outside world.
>
> Beatitudes (MSG)

We continue here to explore stage four and five in the transition process, dealing with *New Beginnings* and *Renewal of Vision*. Once we have found our way across the river, we must locate a suitable place to set up camp to begin a new life of ministry. Debarking and off-loading our gear to locate in a new place requires careful thought and planning. The selection of a campsite in a new place determines the experience. It works best if the whole family is involved and considered in terms of the needs of each as the will of God is sought. Before one can effectively respond to the needs and opportunities of a new place of ministry, it is helpful for personal needs and expectations to be fully explored. There are many options. What do you expect of a place of ministry? What are you bringing with you in terms of your offer of ministry? How well have you articulated what you bring and the nature of the ministry you desire to offer? There are many questions to consider.

Finding one's place in ministry requires some personal exploration and knowledge. Ministry is a broad descriptor. Finding where one fits and discovering what contributes to our fit can help us interface with the opportunities available. Self-understanding involves awareness of one's acquired personality traits, natural abilities, spiritual gifts, strengths, and weaknesses. These all grow out of the developmental working of God's grace in who we are and our opportunities. We are without doubt impacted by the family and culture in which we develop; these too, are gifts of God's grace that provide the opportunities and challenges of our lives. I am reminded of God's response to Jeremiah's questioning of his call: "Before I formed you in the womb I knew you, before you were born I set you apart; I appointed you as a prophet to the nations."

Jeremiah was reluctant: "Ah, Sovereign Lord, I do not know how to speak; I am only a child." Such was Jeremiah's perception of himself.

God rebuked him with this challenge:
"Do not say, 'I am only a child.' You must go to everyone I send you to and say whatever I command you. Do not be afraid of them, for I am with you and will rescue you." Then the Lord touched his mouth and put the words in his mouth and said, "I am watching to see that my word is fulfilled."[39]

We do well to begin with such an experience with God. Frequently, we also need to revise of our understanding of ourselves. This was the experience of so many individuals called of God to be his instruments, throughout biblical history. Moses, Gideon, and many others needed to revise their understanding of themselves and to know God as the one who

---

39 Jeremiah 1:1-19

would continue as the potter, to remould their personalities and enhance their natural abilities with the gifts of his Spirit.

The foundation of our ministry is our relationship with God. But the expression of our ministry goes through the filter of our personality and our natural abilities, complemented by gifts of the Holy Spirit. In this chapter, I want to explore some ways in which we might better understand ourselves and how that may impact our ministry. It is my experience with many pastors that the most opportune time to explore one's identity in ministry is in the midst of the trauma of transition. This is a crisis point at which effective learning can occur because in it we are shaken by anxiety and questioning. These can open us to new vistas.

FROM MANY OPTIONS TO SPECIFICITY

Whether starting out in one's first ministry or transitioning to a new ministry, change grants us the opportunity to create a new beginning. There are many important considerations. Comparison with others can be very distracting, but focusing on God's *personal call* can help us to be specific. The disciples' distraction lay in comparing themselves to each other and questioning the activity of others outside their group. On one occasion they wanted to know who was the greatest among them. Following the Transfiguration of Christ they wanted to stay put instead of going back to the real world of ministry. On yet another occasion they had to face their sense of exclusivity in denying others to do anything in ministry if they were not part of the "in" group. On all such occasions[40] Jesus rebuked his disciples. Consider the contrast of the disciples'

---

40 See Mark 9:34; Luke 9:46; Luke 22:24; Luke 9:49

attitude with that of John the Baptist. John's response when people compared him to his cousin was, "He must become greater; I must become less."[41] John had a clear understanding of his calling and his relationship to Jesus.

This was made more complex when churches (like that in Corinth) preferentially set one preacher over against another.[42] Also, Jesus confronted Peter for expressing more interest in what John was doing than what Jesus had called him to do.[43] It becomes apparent that we are not to get lost in assessing others who are servants of Christ.[44] The Greek words translated *servant* in those two passages to imply two different functions. Paul makes it clear when speaking of roles in ministry that the responsibility of each is to be faithful in the stewardship of their individual calling so that different persons with different personalities and gifts might attend to their own specific duty.

Preparing for and engaging in ministry is unique to each. Moses's preparation included being raised in a surrogate family in Egyptian culture and education, in a rather privileged state. After that he spent forty years in the wilderness nurturing sheep, which may have been a pivotal experience in his preparation for ministry. I wonder if his running away from Egypt had more to do with a fear of his own anger (resulting in murder) than simply a wish to escape punishment. It may have been this that unveiled his true passion for justice and his sense of helplessness to do anything about the situation of the Hebrew people. And rejection by his people may have been a factor. We can only guess as to all that contributed to Moses's self-understanding by the time he experienced the

---

41   John 3:30
42   1 Corinthians 3 and 4
43   John 21:20-23
44   Romans 14 and 1 Corinthians 4

Chapter 6: Finding One's Place in Ministry

call of God. We cannot know the heart of Moses as God did but it would be reasonable to assume that all of these experiences were preparatory to his calling and undoubtedly impacted his ministry.

Jesus spent forty days in the wilderness, during which he faced the temptations of Satan. This test of endurance proved his commitment and his dependence upon the Spirit of God. Being fully man, he experienced temptations common to man, both in the wilderness and later in his public ministry. Paul, after his encounter with Jesus on the road to Damascus spent significant time in the quietness of Arabia. Although we have few details one would expect that it was a time of reflection on his vast knowledge of the Old Testament in a growing awareness of its implications for his new relationship with the Jesus whom he had sought to persecute.

Every pastor, at the beginning of a new ministry, should give himself the sacred gift of quietness in which to contemplatively seek God and understand the relationship between his giftedness and the ministry to which he is called. Moses, when faced with difficult issues, essentially said to the Israelites, "Wait until I find out what the Lord commands concerning you."[45]

It is reasonable to conjecture that God called prophets and leaders in Scripture to specific ministries that required the very giftedness he provided. Many underwent a time to reflect upon and clarify whom they perceived themselves to be and to become assured of God's presence prior to entering public ministry. Most had to deal with doubt and self-questioning in coming to grips with God's call. Many, if not most, were reluctant followers who needed correcting in their

---

45 Numbers 9:6-8

understanding of themselves and of God's role in their ministry. Even today, each individual needs a similar experience.

Foundational questions that must be addressed are as follows: How am I to shape my involvement in ministry? How has God fashioned me for what He has called me to do? What will be the challenges of the world in which I serve or the church, for that matter? The degree to which our culture, family, and society, have influenced us will create major challenges to following a biblical motif. The ways of man are not the ways of God.

We also must integrate our call into the culture of the church where we serve. It is questionable whether it is morally right to go into a church with the intention of dramatically forcing it to conform to us or our particular pattern of ministry unless that was the expected mandate, e.g. when a pastor is assigned to an interim role specifically designed to effect change in the church culture or structure. One pastor accepted a call to a church fully intending to split the church if they did not conform to his particular style. The outcome was that after a couple of years he took those who agreed with him and started a new congregation. This is unacceptable from a Christian perspective. Such action is not much different than marrying with the intent to commandeer a spouse's conformity under the threat of divorce. The greater the transparency in expectations and understanding that exists in the interface between church and pastor, the greater the likelihood of a harmonious outcome.

The understanding that we have of biblical models of ministry will be incarnated in our lives wherever we are placed by God. Daniel and his friends faced this question when they were taken captive to the land of Babylon. "Daniel resolved not to defile himself with royal food and wine."[46] Each person called to minister must face similar questions in terms of the culture in which they serve.

Choosing Among Models

History has spawned many models of ministry, and in our time many more have arisen, each with a label that defines its primary focus: the seeker-sensitive church, the purpose-driven church, the missional church, the real church, the simple church, the New Testament church, and one could name many others. Which model do I fit into? What characteristics of these models are most important in fulfilling the call of God upon my life? Personally, I find elements in each that have appeal. The variation in ministry I have experienced over fifty-five years has opened my mind to a plethora of possibilities. The common thread in the tapestry of my ministry has been to serve people in need (apart from the time of pioneering churches wherein I functioned more as an evangelist). It took several years however, for me to come to a realization of what my specific calling was.

Multiplicity of options requires careful thought and sensitivity to the Holy Spirit as to the place for the expression of God's grace and gifts. Beginning a new ministry is quite different to entering an existing ministry, and in the latter the question of *fit* becomes all-important. The broad range of ministry and leadership models in the Scripture proves that one model does not fit all situations.

---

46 Daniel 1:8

Considering the Context

Daniel ministered in a different context than did King David. Paul ministered in different contexts such as Jerusalem, Corinth, Rome, and many other places. Jesus's style of ministry changed to accommodate those he encountered in Jerusalem, Samaria, or Galilee. Each place of ministry presents its own challenge because of the different people involved, the demographic and culture of the community, and varying ministry opportunities. Nehemiah served in a very different context under King Artaxerxes than when he was rebuilding walls in Jerusalem under all the distractions created by the opposition of Sanballat. A pastor engaged in a building project has a different ministry than a person serving the aged or a chaplain ministering to a transient crowd in an airport. Jeremiah's labour was different than Hosea's, and Paul functioned in quite different ways on his first visit to Ephesus than he did on later visits. We have a considerable responsibility to adjust to the context into which we are called.

It is incumbent upon a pastor to analyze and adjust as congregational needs change. A church in conflict calls for a healing ministry that may be very different to a congregation that has plateaued at a level of ineffectiveness or stagnation. One pattern does not fit all. The best time to research and identify the particular needs of a congregation is during the initial invitation to a new ministry. Mutual understanding of expectations early on saves much tension later.

If the relationship between pastor and congregation can be viewed as a covenant before God to seek his will for the ministry, a firm base is established for the relationship. The vision that grows out of that clarification will bring focus to one's ministry in regard to the pastor's gifts and the needs of the congregation.

Exploring Giftedness

A considerable degree of harmony must exist between the specific needs of a congregation, the spiritual gifts of a pastor and the gifts of church members. There is a story of a man who played his acoustic guitar by consistently plucking one string on one fret. The sound was singular and constant. His wife, in visiting some friends, saw a man playing his guitar, using all of the strings and running his fingers up and down the frets. She came home excited to share this new way of doing things. His confident response was, "Don't worry, dear, he will do better when he finds the right note!" Both pastors and churches need to take care that they do not get stuck plucking on just one string.

The Spirit of God gives pastors a range of gifts but probably not all at the same level of expertise. A pastor needs all the strings on his guitar, plus the skill to play the proper note in a given situation. No one should presume to have all the gifts required in any given ministry. It is important to identify each person's gifting and how those gifts may most effectively be used.[47] There are certain gifts quite specific to pastoring such as teaching, edification, and nurturing, but a pastor may also be gifted in administration or leadership. Some will be gifted in evangelism, wisdom in problem-solving, motivation of others, or in creative visioning. Paul identified gifts in his coworkers and encouraged them to help others resolve various points of conflict.[48] Barnabas was gifted in encouragement and Epaphroditus was gifted with compassion and perseverance. Paul consulted with leaders in Jerusalem so as to draw upon their wisdom and intimate knowledge of the Lord.

---

47   1 Corinthians 12:12-31; Ephesians 4:7-13
48   See Philippians 4:2-3

Different opinions abound about spiritual gifts. My desire is to emphasize a few basic principles. Spiritual gifts are given by God and harmonized in the body of Christ through the ministry of the Holy Spirit. Their intended use is to help, edify and strengthen church members as they evidence the presence of God among us. We are to seek to excel in those gifts that build up the church. They are to bring much blessing to the recipient but their overriding purpose is to edify the church and witness to unbelievers.[49]

In one Christian organization, our first step was to determine a vision for one of its departments of ministry. Once that vision became clear, we identified the roles necessary for achieving that ministry. A third step was to list the spiritual gifts necessary. Then in seeking leadership and participants, we assessed the gifting of applicants commensurate to our need and hired suitable staff. There was not always a perfect fit. It was necessary to provide additional training and development for individuals to complete the skills and abilities required for a successful ministry. This process achieved the needed range of giftedness in the ministry team assembled for that particular ministry. Everyone cannot play first base! Each member's awareness of the giftedness of others created an opportunity for communal support and interdependence within the group. The resulting synergism produced an effective ministry.

Let's Get Personal

Discerning one's God-given giftedness and natural abilities is a complicated task. This journey into self-awareness is a sacred

---

49   1 Corinthians 12-14

journey.[50] However, as one begins the journey it is necessary to understand that self-awareness cannot rely simply on self-assessment. There are several helpful places in which to find assistance. An absolute necessity is openness to personal input from others. Paul frequently identified the abilities and gifting of those he commended to churches for ministry. Input from godly people who speak with wisdom is an excellent source for help, and this may include family members, teachers, or pastors who have observed us during our developing years. They may discern God at work in our lives. Also, opening ourselves to an intimate relationship with God is essential. The Psalmist cried, "Search me, O God, and know my heart."[51] God used the prophet Nathan to bring David to awareness of himself.[52] Other spiritual helpers may help us to know ourselves.

Caution is advised in self-assessment; our self-perception may be distorted by either negativity or pride. This sacred voyage requires that we set our sails to catch the wind of the Spirit in the quietness of our inner world. And we can look to our giftedness for guidance as to God's will in our quest to know ourselves and our place in ministry. Who you are is God's gift to you! What you do with who you are is your gift to him!

The emphasis in our culture is on individualism, and this makes it easy to misunderstand the role of the community of faith in discerning the will of God for our lives. Scottish theologian, John Baillie, observes, "We must at once remind

---

50 David G. Benner, *The Gift of Being Yourself: the Sacred Call to self-discovery* (Downers Grove: InterVarsity Press, 20004) and Frederick Buechner, *Telling Secrets*, (New York,NY: HarperCollins, 1992) and Buechner, *Sacred Journey*, (New York, NY: HarperCollins, 1882). These are helpful books.
51 Psalm 139:23
52 2 Samuel 12

ourselves that it is not to the individual Christian in his solitude that God reveals himself, but to the faithful community, and to the individual only in community."[53] I am sure there have been exceptions to this generalized statement; however, in our culture it is easy to overlook our need for embeddedness in community. If we have grown up in a community of faith there is a good chance the wise adults in that community know us well. If we wish to know ourselves as God knows us, it is important to look through several windows to achieve a comprehensive picture of God's manifest grace in our lives.

Why Professional Testing?

It is important for a skilled craftsman to know his tools and the specific use of each instrument that he will use in his creative work. My hobby of carving in wood requires simple knives, complex chisels, and sanding equipment. One might consider their abilities and gifts as the tools that God has provided for creatively bringing people in artistic fashion into the kingdom of God and helping them to spiritual maturity.

The behavioural sciences offer specific tests designed to assist in identifying abilities, qualities of personality, and coping skills for vocational assessment. I have had the privilege of providing psychological and vocational testing for several thousand individuals engaged in ministry. Many mission organizations require such testing for overseas deployment, and this would be just as helpful for pastors. These instruments have proven to be most helpful in guiding individuals into a ministry that can effectively use their gifts and abilities.

---

53 Baillie, John, *The Sense of the Presence of God* (London: Oxford University Press, 1992) p.92

Personality testing identifies relationship variables, family dynamics, and capacity to cope with stress, as well as leadership and management styles. Other testing focuses on vocational functioning. Such information is not only beneficial to the individual but also to those responsible for the placement of persons in ministry. These instruments, when used in conjunction with a clear understanding of spiritual dimensions, can be very useful.

My training was in the use of personality testing, clinical testing, vocational testing and testing to identify resources for coping with stress. Because of the large scope of this topic, I will discuss only a couple of the most pertinent here, focusing on those that I have found best for persons involved in the process of transition.

All professional testing is well researched, standardized, and designed for a high level of reliability. Many such instruments are based upon self-reporting through the use of multiple choice or preferences of the person. With respect to ministry personnel, extensive research has indicated that marital, family, spiritual, and organizational variables significantly impact one's performance and effectiveness in ministry.[54] My involvement in the lives of scores of pastors in transition reflects the same conclusion.

For me, the instrument of choice in dealing with pastors in transition has been the Highlands Ability Battery (HAB) developed by the Highlands Company.[55] It was specifically

---

54 Andrews, L.A., ed., *The Family in Mission: Understanding and Caring for Those Who Serve,* (Colorado Springs, CO: Mission Training International, 2004) and Powell and Bowers, eds., *Enhancing Missionary Vitality,* (Colorado Springs, CO: Mission Training International, 2002). Some of my work in research and writing is found each of these books.

55 For more information see: www.highlandsco.com

designed to match one's natural abilities with career choices and to assist youth in choosing the focus of their academic career and adults in mid-career choices and changes. Rather than depend upon self-reporting, the HAB consists of exercises performed to measure *functional ability*. Functional ability identifies what a person's natural abilities are and which ones bring fulfillment and satisfaction through their expression. What gives us joy and fulfillment in doing relates to natural abilities. I would add that my experience is that joy is also experienced in expressing God's gifts of grace.

It is important to understand that the HAB differentiates between *natural abilities* and *skills*. Intelligence enables us through practice, to develop skills whereas the expression of natural abilities is much more intuitive. Skills express *acquired* functions whereas we are *born* with natural abilities. One might say natural abilities are the way we are wired. In their totality, they demonstrate our uniqueness and individuality. Of course, acquired skills also add to our uniqueness as individuals.

The completion of the HAB battery of exercises ascertains one's natural abilities by the degree to which the exercises are completed in a limited time. The fact that this battery can be completed via computer is a large plus. The ability profile identifies characteristics such as personal style, driving abilities, specialized abilities, and vocabulary. Driving abilities are those that appear to have an internal push for their expression. The results compare a person's scores with others who fit the same demographic. The results of the HAB are categorized in terms of learning channels (which are the style by which we learn best), problem-solving abilities, communication, preferred work environment, and the type of work for which one's abilities would best suit them. These factors uncover our natural propensity for inductive or deductive reasoning, our spatial abilities (which enable us to conceptualize in two or three dimensions), our idea productivity, and our verbal and number memory. Our most natural relational style is clearly identified as well as our planning abilities.

One can readily see how such information would be helpful to a person seeking to understand how God has equipped him for ministry. It also opens the way for understanding how God's giftedness fits one for ministry opportunities. This has proven beneficial to pastors who are entering into new beginnings and renewing their vision of ministry, following the transition out of a previous ministry or simply rewriting one's ministry plan in a continuing ministry. It provides some clarity in prioritizing ministry options.

As illustrated in the diagram following, there are seven contributing elements to the achievement of our goals. This rather simple diagram illustrates how the HAB conceives of natural abilities fitting into the process of developing vocational goals. Along with family and values, natural abilities are foundational. Based on this foundation, we build a personal style and develop a large range of skills—many of which may not be an expression of our natural abilities. These skills are learned and acquired through intelligence and practice. Interests are developed and work experiences gained as we mature and are exposed to expanding opportunities. They develop in adulthood with the setting of vocational goals as we move toward a life of accomplishment and productivity.

<u>GOALS</u>
⬆
<u>INTERESTS</u> <u>WORK CYCLE</u>
⬆
<u>PERSONAL STYLE</u> <u>SKILLS</u>
⬆
<u>FAMILY</u> <u>NATURAL ABILITIES</u> <u>VALUES</u>

From a Christian point of view I would add that the experience of God's grace and giftedness is an absolute necessity in ministry. Our personal style of relating, coupled with skills learned through education and work are expressed in our interests and choices of ministry. HAB research indicates that it is in the expression of natural abilities, coupled with opportunities consistent with one's values, that life finds its maximum satisfaction and fulfillment. One cannot avoid dealing with the impact of one's family and their positive affirmation or negative response to one's vocational choice. In ministry that is fulfilling, we will express natural abilities, values, personal style, skills, and interests directed toward the work of the ministry and its goals.

You may have noticed that people exercising their natural abilities often experience more joy than someone performing a task simply because job or duty requires it. A greater sense of fulfillment is experienced in expressing natural abilities compared to using skills unrelated to natural abilities.

But not all of the skills we develop are necessarily related to our natural abilities or our giftedness. Personal style is shaped much by our family and the cultural input we experienced as we were growing up. Our new life in Christ requires that we bring our personal style into line with the behaviour that Christ demonstrated in his earthly life. The Scriptures tell us that God knew Jeremiah before he was born. It is a reasonable deduction that our God-given natural abilities are an outcome of his sovereign involvement in our coming into this world, as are our gifts in the Holy Spirit. It is equally important to add to this our spiritual growth in Christ, which involves maturing in him and obeying his call to ministry. Based upon the theological foundations of our self-understanding and the enabling of God's grace in our lives, I would conclude that there can be a synergism between what I achieve in self-knowledge both through assessment tools and the operation of God's grace in my life.

In the following chapter other dimensions of biblical teaching will be presented so as to further explore how we may enter into new ministry opportunities with improved self-awareness.

> In your love you kept me... you have put all my sins behind your back...
> The Lord will save me, and we will sing with stringed instruments all the days of our lives in the temple of the Lord.
>
> Isaiah 38:17-20

QUESTIONS FOR REFLECTION

The *place* of ministry should provide the opportunity for a pastor to exercise his gifts and abilities. Did you feel that your past experience created such an opportunity? How well do you know your abilities and gifts and how they may best be exercised in ministry? Have you explored different ministry models as presented in your culture and in the Scripture? What models appear to fit your abilities and gifts best?

Chapter Seven

Perspectives on One's Role in Ministry

> You're blessed when you can show people how to cooperate instead of compete or fight. That's when you discover who you really are, and your place in God's family.
>
> Beatitudes (MSG)

One shoe does not fit all, or to put it the other way about, every foot does not properly fit one shoe. Equally, one ministry does not fit all nor does everyone fit into one type of ministry. In chapter six, it was noted that there are many different ministries to which God calls individuals and the models of ministry today are legion. The different ministries utilize a variety of gifts and abilities. Now we will explore the degree of flexibility associated with finding one's specific role as a servant of God. Continuing my camping analogy, diverse expectations lead to selecting different camping places. No one camping place fulfills the need of every camper.

Abilities, Gifts, and Personality

Differences in personality, abilities, giftedness and capacity to deal with varying levels of stress in ministry are abundantly illustrated in the biblical stories. Determining one's fit into a specific opportunity is complex. In these choices, we are dependent upon the call of God and the placement of God.

It is clear from Scripture that gifts are given not only for the benefit of the recipient alone, but also for the edification of the community of faith and the glory of God. Divine wisdom from the Holy Spirit and the wisdom of spiritual mentors is of great importance. Professional testing has proven useful but should not be seen as an answer in and of itself.

An important consideration is the fact that we change as we pass through the stages of life.[56] Pastors do not leap full grown from the womb but continue to mature after being called. Life stages impact ministry. The passing of years and growth that comes with maturing brings changes to our involvement in ministry. Acknowledging this reality opens us to a re-assessment of our function in ministry as we mature. Frequently, pastors who begin their ministry in working with youth, or other specialized ministry, find that they reach a stage where it is important to re-define their ministry. It is not uncommon for individuals to re-adjust their ministry role after twelve to eighteen years. This redefinition is common for those in secular employment also. For some, the first few years in ministry are a time of discovery and refinement of their particular gifts. Others continue in the same type of ministry through their entire journey. Either way, assessment from time to time is both helpful and entirely appropriate. It is best viewed as an opportunity to achieve greater harmony between one's abilities, gifts, and ministry opportunities.

---

56   This topic is discussed by the following two authors. Charles M. Sell, *Transitions Through Adult Life* (Grand Rapids, MI: Zondervan, 1985, 1991) and Tim Stafford, *As Our Years Increase* (Grand Rapids: Zondervan, 1989)

Chapter 7: Perspectives on One's Role in Ministry

As churches grow, their needs change. Sometimes pastors mature beyond the opportunities of a given situation and sometimes churches grow beyond the capacity of a particular pastor to meet their needs. Acknowledging this may lead to the hiring of multiple pastors. To illustrate: Archie was greatly blessed with growth in the church where he served. He became overwhelmed and frustrated that he could not meet all the demands. He embarked on a process of determining the areas of his giftedness and how his gifts might best be expressed. Many demands were outside of his comfort zone. When he told his elders what he felt called to do and what was beyond his calling, they immediately affirmed his observations and recommended finding a second pastor whose gifts would complement those of Archie. As the church grew the number of pastors increased. They went on to create a team of individuals who would enhance each other's strengths and focus in ministry.

Team ministry dramatically changes the role of each pastor and necessitates quality in team leadership. It requires each leader to learn to function as a member of a team rather than independently. Much conflict arises if a lead pastor does not have the skills to develop a team milieu with other associates on a pastoral team. Frequently, this has been a key contributor to pastors needing counselling. Coordinating a team is quite different to being a sole pastor. Among pastors with whom I have counselled who work in teams, the most common contributor to dissatisfaction has been the absence of team affirmation. The team leader must be an active participant in the lives of team members. His role model should be Paul who constantly affirmed, encouraged, comforted, and provided freedom of personal self-direction to those who were his fellow labourers. Moses needed the intervention of Jethro to see the need for others to stand with him.

The absence of a team leader's role in the life of a team may be justified with many rationalizations such as giving others freedom, not being over-controlling or dictatorial. In many situations, these justifications have been expressed by team leaders who were never trained in team leadership. Sometimes, they have been loners. Occasionally, more authoritarian lead pastors function in an excessively controlling manner that destroys much potential inherent in team opportunities.

The function of a team leader is the stewardship of those whom God has placed under his leadership. Leadership is not simply an exercise of authority. A study of Paul's use of his authority is instructive. He claims to have authority equal to that of the other apostles. However, he claims the primary function of his authority is to build up others.[57] He does not function in an authoritarian way in relation to his fellow workers.

In pioneering new churches, the pastoral role is essentially that of an evangelist and motivator. But as new believers come into the church, that role changes, for now the need is to disciple people to maturity. In one ministry that focused on reaching street youth, the needs of the youth changed dramatically after they professed faith in Christ. Scores of new believers who had no background or understanding of what it meant to be a Christian were soon in need of pastoral ministry to help them learn Christian values and understand the implications of their new commitment. Workers who were very effective in street work proved not to be very effective in mentoring new believers. And as there was no wish to curtail their work on the street it became necessary to hire a pastor for those who had newly come to faith. This required a person with pastoral gifts of care and nurture who also had

---

57 2 Corinthians 10:8 and 13:10

the skill to confront the challenges of spiritual growth among street youth.

For this reason it is important for pastors to initiate some helpful reassessment as they move through the years of ministry. God is presented in Scripture as exercising stewardship over those whom he calls. He administers his grace according to his plan for each of us. Paul states, "You have heard about the administration of God grace that was given to me for you."[58] Administration or stewardship is a term of management. God clearly transfers the responsibility of managing and administering his grace in our lives into our hands to a large extent. Paul speaks of this as a "trust committed to me."[59] "Those who have been given a trust must prove faithful."[60]

Paul is very clear concerning our responsibility to be good stewards of our gifts in the service of God's kingdom. It is an awesome responsibility but it is not solely an individual one. Our peers in ministry, denominational leaders and the community of faith play a significant role. We need to take up the task of helping one another find our unique function as a member of the body. Paul helped many to fulfill their ministry. The example of the church in deciding to set aside Barnabas and Paul for their ministry is a worthy model. Paul managed his team of his fellow workers with generosity and exercised his influence with relational sensitivity. He constantly promoted the work of others. He evidenced no desire for control over those engaged with him. In fact, he declared that he had authority but chose not to use it except to

---

58   Ephesians 3:2
59   1 Corinthians 9:17; Colossians 1:25; 1 Timothy 1:4; Ephesians 3:2. The word is oikonomia: stewardship
60   1 Corinthians 4:2; Titus 1:7; 1 Peter 4:10. The word is oikonomos: steward

discipline the doctrinally unsound or those who had breached moral standards.

It is important for each of us to see the relationship between our personality characteristics, our natural abilities, and the spiritual gifts, which have such prominence in the New Testament. There is no conflict between natural abilities and gifts of the Holy Spirit. It is my conviction and observation that there is a high degree of correlation between them.

On the other hand, patterns of relationship and personality characteristics developed in our maturing process may conflict with both our natural abilities and our giftedness. I am suggesting that abilities, spiritual gifts, and personality traits can be distinguished from one from the other. The fact that they are integrated in each person is obvious. Natural abilities are presumed to be rather fixed by the teen years and consist of functional capacities that come naturally. An example may help: many people express natural gifts in music (which we often refer to as "playing by ear") whereas others acquire skills in music through prolonged practice. This natural ability is clearly different than a learned skill. Personality traits are learned responses developed in the relational context of our family and culture. Personality may be defined as a constellation of behaviour patterns. The Scriptures clearly identify many behaviour patterns as coming from our fallen nature. They are in need of transformation by God's grace and are to be replaced by behaviour that demonstrates our new life in Christ. The more a ministry creates opportunity for the integration of natural abilities and skills the more one will experience fulfillment. Personality traits must be brought into conformity to Christ, which requires God's grace and the sanctifying ministry of the Holy Spirit.

In our culture, personality has come to be viewed as both autonomous and sacrosanct. People will claim the right to be whoever they believe themselves to be. Personality is a constellation of behavioural patterns that express themselves in relationships. They were learned and developed in a family and cultural context and are not solely the choice or the creation of their possessor. A spoiled child does not make the choice alone to be obnoxious and belligerent or to be a bully or to be submissive or self-effacing. These qualities develop in a complicated relational context. They become patterns of behaviour that impact one's functioning as an adult and are sufficiently imbedded in one's personality as to inhibit the expression of one's abilities and values. We become what we are in our community and should not justify our behaviour as simply "the way we are."

Moses's developed personality traits led him to express his anger in murdering an Egyptian. The self-perception that led him to resist the call of God was neither consistent with his natural abilities nor the gifts of grace that God wished to express in him. Similarly, Jeremiah's perception of himself as a child did not correspond to God's perception of him. He too, needed the touch of God. Gideon assumed the limitations he attributed to his tribe of origin. Joseph manifested abilities and gifts as a child that in adulthood matured into outstanding leadership.

It is incumbent upon us to acknowledge and celebrate both our natural abilities and the gifts of the Holy Spirit. There is danger in assuming we have the right to hold to our acquired understanding of ourselves. It is also necessary for us to address those failing dimensions of personality and interpersonal functioning that issue from our fallen nature and from growing up in a less than perfect world. We must pursue maturity in Christ until the life of Christ becomes manifest in our lives. Personality is not something we are born with. Abilities develop and attitudes form. God in his grace desires to make us much more than we are; when he calls, he also equips.

Emotional Intelligence and Learning Agility

In recent years our understanding of intelligence and its impact on our behaviour has changed. Intelligence is being rethought from a number of different perspectives. Rod Wilson, President of Regent College, Vancouver, discussed *emotional intelligence* in a presentation at the college entitled, "Why is Emotional Intelligence Missing in So many Churches and Christian Institutions?"[61] His question was provoked by the evidence that pastors sometimes display a "lack of self-awareness and inadequate relational abilities." He went on to discuss intelligence and its testing.

Wilson suggests "EQ (is) one aspect of intelligence that enables us to deal with the vicissitudes of life." It is defined in academic literature as a cognitive ability that, in reality, is mixed with aspects of personality and reasoning. Other research defines EQ as involving self-awareness, self-regulation, motivation, empathy, and social skills.[62] Thus, EQ is all about management and awareness of self in a social context where relationships are nurtured through inspirational leadership, influence, conflict management, and teamwork. Wil-

---

61 Available at www.regent-college.edu presented in 2011.
62 Valarie Duncan, *The Heart of Leadership: Thoughts on Identifying, Recruiting and Developing Emotional Intelligence to Enhance Organizational Effectiveness*, (Highlands Forum Quarterly, July, 2010) available to members at www.highlandsco.com.

son discusses this from a theological perspective in terms of our understanding of the Trinity and our experience of the incarnate Christ.

To better understand this, one must explore the role of emotion. The centrality of empathy, compassion, encouragement, and love as expressed in the ministry of Jesus is well worthy of detailed study and imitation by pastors. Paul clearly defines the qualities of godly relationships and commends these to pastors and other leaders in the churches. It is not appropriate to neglect these qualities because they do not come naturally to us. The behaviour of love is the essence of biblical emotional intelligence and constitutes much of the job description of the servant of God.[63]

Another area discussed today is social intelligence, which focuses the importance of relational sensitivity and skills leading to interpersonal effectiveness. Obviously, this is a key to the expression of pastoral relationships that will be transformative in the lives of people. Relational sensitivity is a foundational quality of leadership.

Yet another area of recent study is *learning agility*, which is discussed in terms of the need for leaders to be "flexible, adaptable, and welcoming of the challenging situations at hand."[64] This nimbleness and creativity focuses on the ability to respond to challenging, changing situations with creativity in process and goal identification. These qualities can be nurtured intentionally, leading to openness to new ideas and the development of one's imagination. They are further enhanced by brainstorming and exposing oneself to different opinions and perspectives. Knowing one's particular style of learning

---

63 1 Timothy 6:11ff, Titus 2:1-8
64 Eric D. Chick, *Learning Agility: the Key Ingredient for Effective Leadership in Turbulent Times* (Highlands Forum Quarterly, April, 2010).

is important since we all develop preferences for learning in personal ways. It has been quite revealing for some pastors to discover that their ability to learn through *listening* exceeds their ability to learn through *reading*. Accordingly, developing learning agility increases leadership effectiveness as one develops their natural abilities and flexibility. Learning agility is expressed in creativity and idea productivity. Intelligence contributes less to creativity than do other factors that facilitate innovative thinking.

Research on emotional intelligence and leadership agility is simply an attempt to better understand what creates effective leadership and ministry. Consider biblical leaders who were both creative and agile in addressing problems creatively. Joseph became a great example of leadership, manifesting both emotional intelligence and leadership agility while very consciously remaining aware of God in his every step. Solomon was given wisdom from God that demonstrated both qualities. Nehemiah was a great example of emotional intelligence, leadership agility, and spiritual wisdom not only in his relationship with Artaxerxes but also in his administrative leadership in re-building the wall. Certainly, Moses is another example of a person who later matured into a leader who exemplified these qualities. Daniel combined emotional intelligence, learning agility, and spiritual wisdom with a humility that led to his placement in top leadership in a godless culture. Paul matured into these qualities as he walked with Christ to fulfill his call in ministry. The grace of God and the enabling of the Holy Spirit was what brought about these qualities in biblical leaders.

We may often limit ourselves in the accomplishment of God's purposes by the limitations of our self-perception. Of the twelve who explored the Promised Land only two could see God's hand at work; others became stuck in the view they had from the mirror of their own self-understanding.[65] The report concerning the land and the giants was accurate; however, Caleb and Joshua could see the need to venture in faith that God would keep his promise. A contrary majority vote led the Israelites to turn away only to end up wandering in the desert. Majority decisions are not the right ones when God is left out of the equation. The perspective that caused defeat was, "We seemed like grasshoppers in our own eyes, and we looked the same to them."[66] A faulty perception of God and the fear of man caused them to see themselves as grasshoppers, to rebel and reject God's offer of success in occupying the land. We must choose between perceiving ourselves as grasshoppers and seeing ourselves from a grace-perspective enabled and equipped by God's grace.

Paul was very conscious of the fact that the foundation of his ministry was the grace of God, and not the excellent qualifications of his religious upbringing or best of education of the day.[67] Unfortunately, in our day education is often seen as the key foundation for ministry preparation rather than the quality of one's relationship with God. We would all benefit from revising our self-perception with a view to God fulfilling his desires through us. From the above discussion, it is evident that many things contribute to understanding one's potential for ministry. Achieving such understanding is critical if one is to interact with God's call to ministry.

---

65   Numbers 13:1-33 and Deuteronomy 1:19-45
66   Numbers 13:33
67   Acts 22:3; Philippians 3:4-10; 2 Corinthians 11:5

THE POETRY OF GOD

In the New Testament God is declared to have two poems. Paul uses the Greek word *poiyma* in Romans and Ephesians.[68] In Romans, it refers to creation, or, *what has been made*. Simply put, creation is God's poem. The Psalmist recorded a similar thought: "The skies proclaim the work of his hands."[69] Paul was convinced that much could be known of God by studying what he has created. His "eternal power and divine nature" may be clearly seen through his creativity in bringing order out chaos.

The work of *our* hands reveals much about us. If we think of the artist, writer, or craftsman, it is easy to see how character, values, and interests are expressed in their work. These qualities are also expressed in our ministry. In the Ephesian passage,[70] the word *poiyma* is translated "workmanship" or "masterpiece." We are called "God's workmanship, created in Christ Jesus to do good works which God prepared in advance for us to do." Because we are part of God's creation, we are his poem. As a result of his saving grace we have become individually and corporately, his masterpiece. Paul writes, "By the grace of God I am what I am, and his grace to me was not without effect. No, I worked harder than all of them—yet not I, but the grace of God that was with me."[71]

This is emphasized in many other passages. For example, "Surely you have heard about the administration of God's grace that was given to me for you,"[72] declares Paul. Entering ministry with a grace perspective is an excellent place to start.

---

68   Romans 1:20 and Ephesians 2:10
69   Psalm 19:1
70   Ephesians 2:10
71   1 Corinthians 15:10
72   See: 1 Peter 4:10; 1 Corinthians 3:10; Ephesians 3:2,7

Perhaps you have never thought of yourself as a poem of God but clearly, he sees you as his creation, both in your natural and spiritual gifts.

Exploring Weaknesses

Paul was engaged in his ministry as a man of his culture, upbringing, and education. His ministry was in fact a partnership of sorts between his humanness and the God he chose to serve. He had to live and deal with the reality of his past, and he was not hesitant to acknowledge the benefits and liabilities of his past. He re-evaluated both from the perspective of his new relationship with Christ. Moses and Gideon were very conscious of their limitations and weaknesses as they understood them. We too, need to be aware of what we bring to our encounter with God.

The New Testament deals with this matter explicitly. Let me direct your attention to what is said about weaknesses. First, in the book of Hebrews we read, "For we do not have a high priest who is unable to sympathize with our weaknesses, but we have one who has been tempted in every way, just as we are—yet was without sin."[73] Jesus understands and sympathizes with our weaknesses. Secondly, the Holy Spirit "helps in our weakness."[74] If we expand the word *help* considering the composition of the word, we would read, "The Holy Spirit, at his initiative, constantly comes over beside us and together with us takes hold of our weakness." We are not left alone but have the constant support of the Spirit.

---

73   Hebrews 4:15
74   Romans 8:26

Thirdly, we are also told "we who are strong ought to bear with the weaknesses of the weak and not to please ourselves."[75] I might add that the word *bear* means to carry away and to put up with or comprehend. Fourthly, Paul writes[76] that God's grace is sufficient and in weakness he finds the strength God supplies to be sufficient. The adequacy of God's grace gives assurance that what we cannot change about ourselves does not inhibit him from accomplishing his purposes in us. Fifthly, we have the wonderful examples in Scripture of men and women of faith "whose weaknesses were turned to strength" through the power of faith in God.[77] The power of God in response to their faith so significantly overshadowed their weaknesses that their lives of faith glorified him.

We too, need to strive to remove every hindrance in ourselves whether those are weaknesses, personality traits, or behaviour patterns and to do so by the grace and enabling of the Holy Spirit. The control we seek is not simply discipline but the power of God manifest in our lives. The energizing of God's Spirit accesses the "incomparably great power for us who believe."[78] We should seek to serve in that grace. Our part is to cooperate with him in dealing with, eliminating, learning from, and transforming our weaknesses through every effort we can muster. We know that we have this "treasure in jars of clay to show that this all-surpassing power is from God and not of us."[79] In this context, we recognize that wherever God calls us, he can surely enable us to accomplish his

---

75   Romans 15:1
76   2 Corinthians 11-30-12:10
77   Hebrews 11:34
78   Ephesians 1:15-23
79   2 Corinthians 4:7

intended purposes. Ministry begun from this perspective will approach each obstacle with faith.

Surprised by the Call

In the Scriptures most people who were called to serve God expressed surprise. This was true of Moses, Gideon, Jeremiah, Esther, Isaiah, and Paul. It may be that each of the disciples was equally surprised as Matthew, when Jesus invited him to be a disciple. I can personally identify with that surprise. If someone had suggested to me as a youth that God would call me to the ministry that has occupied me for the past sixty years, I would have thought they were hallucinating.

Being surprised at God's call often issues from a sense of inadequacy. It is a case of our not feeling we have the capacity for such service. Of course, when called, we have little comprehension of the capacity of God's grace for our lives. We may feel the inadequacy of Moses, the immaturity of Jeremiah, the inferiority of Gideon or the fear of Esther in response to God's invitation. Quite obviously, there is little certainty that our self-perception corresponds to the way God sees us. The ministry of each of these patriarchs and what God accomplished in them stands in stark contrast to their perception of themselves.

Responding to the call of God requires that we believe he is able to energize us by his Spirit, to accomplish his will in our lives. We must have hearts that are open to transforming growth by his enabling. Paul speaks of this in writing to Timothy, "I thank Christ Jesus our Lord, who has given me strength, that he considered me faithful, appointing me to his service."[80] We bring what we have just as Moses brought his dead staff, to be made alive by the power of God. We come to serve, not as who we are, but as the person we can become by his grace. We are dependent upon his strength.

Paul's prayer is instructive: "Since the day we heard about you, we have not stopped praying for you and asking God to fill you with the knowledge of his will through all spiritual understanding. And we pray this in order that you may live a life worthy of the Lord…growing in the knowledge of God, being strengthened with all power according to his glorious might so that you may have great endurance and patience, and joyfully giving thanks to the Father."[81] Abram the risk-taker became Abraham the man whose faith was credited as righteousness.[82] Jacob the deceiver became Israel, the man who saw God's face.[83] Esther the timid became the one to rescue God's people from death. Saul the persecutor became Paul, the one who took the Gospel of grace to the Gentiles.

Are we willing to be transformed in character and giftedness to become effective instruments in the hand of God? We need to know who we are and what we bring to the call of God. We also need an open heart to become what God desires us to be. What an amazing adventure in grace! After her redemption from Egypt, Israel's story of failure became God's story of love and faithfulness. So also *our story* of ministry is to become *his story* of grace and transformation.

---

80   1 Timothy 1:12, see also Philippians 4:13 and 2 Timothy 4:17
81   Colossians 1:9-12
82   Genesis 15:6
83   Genesis 32:22-32

Clarifying One's Commitment in Ministry

The decision to enter ministry must correspond to the call of God. At an individual level, each person must explore what that call means. It is wise to seek the input of others who have an understanding of ministry. The degree to which one couples self-awareness with guidance from others and from the Lord is a firm predictor of the likelihood of finding the place of most effective ministry. This is not a time to go it alone. In the end, one must decide for oneself what their ministry will be. The clarification of one's commitment is foundational. It is important to be able to articulate this call for oneself and for others upon entering into any ministry. The principle simply stated is: Clarify your commitment before the test of circumstance. This is a biblical principle. In many denominations ordination involves a communal recognition and affirmation of this call.

This requires thinking ahead and planning one's responses to avoid reactivity in volatile situations. Many problems can be anticipated. When Daniel and his three friends were taken into captivity, they clarified their commitment with a resolution that they would not defile themselves, but would remain faithful to Jehovah.[84] Having clarified their commitment, they decided on an alternative suggestion which they courteously offered to the chief officials. This is negotiation at its best. That clarification of their commitment, I believe, played a very large role in the account of the fiery furnace. The time to make a decision is not when you are standing in front of the blazing furnace! Prior clarification and commitment enabled them to remain faithful, and God in his grace freed them to dance in the flames.

---

84   Daniel 1:6-21

This truth is also illustrated by Jesus in Gethsemane where he wrestled in agony to clarify his commitment. "Your will be done," was his conclusion.[85] He then confronted the crowd with authority manifesting dignity and strength during his arrest and trial. Paul did not enter into his ministry with ambiguity concerning his call but took time aside in Arabia. This was likely a time of similar clarification. Peter listened when encountered by God in a dream that enabled him to respond appropriately to the request to Cornelius. In history, we have many examples of great pioneers in missions and other ministries who took time to consider the price of their commitment and, as a result, were able to endure in the most trying circumstances. We must follow in the train of these saints who have gone before us.

It is my conviction that many of the disturbing and anxiety-inducing issues of church ministry can be obviated if we clarify our commitment before we encounter trying circumstances. The elimination of knee-jerk reactionary responses would enable us to avoid many words that should never be spoken and many actions that we later regret. One may speak of this process as creating a *philosophy of practice* in ministry: contemplating the options available, examining oneself and an understanding of the context in which one may most effectively fulfill God's calling. The inventory of personal abilities, liabilities, giftedness by God, and capacity to cope with the stress of ministry is all relevant in considering ministry opportunities available. This is a major undertaking. One must be open to ongoing exploration of personal development and change. An open mind and creativity is needed as we respond to the challenges, all the while depending upon God's guidance and enabling.

---

85 Matthew 26:36-46; Mark 14:32-42; Luke 22:39-45

The Lord is the everlasting God, the creator of the
   ends of the earth.
He will not grow tired or weary, and his understanding no one can fathom.
He gives strength to the weary and increases the
   power of the weak...
Those who hope in the Lord will renew their strength.

Isaiah 40:28-31

QUESTIONS FOR REFLECTION

Do you feel that you are open to exploring your past with a view to understanding how it impacts your present? Are there ways you could revise your self-perception to free you for more effective relationships or ministry? Identify a peer with whom you would be comfortable to explore any of the considerations raised in this chapter. Are you surprised by God's call? Are there clarifications that you could make in your understanding of your call to ministry that would assist in choices you make or how you communicate with others?

Chapter Eight

Meeting the Challenges of Ministry

> You're blessed when your commitment to God provokes persecution.
> The persecution drives you even deeper into God's kingdom.
>
> Beatitudes (MSG)

The challenges of ministry vary with each situation. These challenges may come from outside the community of faith, such as the persecution that led to the dispersal of the apostles following the death of Stephen. They may arise from within, such as was experienced in the conflict that came from the complaint of the Grecian Jews. Challenges are a constant. Paul defined his ministry in terms of his stewardship of the grace of God, to which he was determined to be faithful. He experienced the pressures of leadership. Beyond this the burden of compassion for the people he served and the churches that became communities of faith in an unaccepting culture was heavy on him. Challenges will vary from pastor to pastor but many of the pressures Paul experienced will be common to every ministry. Every pastor must respond to the expectations of a congregation and its members including the interplay of these expectations with his own sense of call.

The Challenges of Leadership

The call to ministry is personal but it is not separate from the community of faith. It is important to understand the relationship between pastor and people as presented in Scripture. Some writing on church leadership takes models for leadership from the Old Testament. This approach has its limitations. Leadership in the Old Testament was expressed primarily in that of the prophet, priest, king, and judge. Other leaders were called to specific tasks that did not fit those categories. The prophet role in the New Testament appears to be diffused through the body of believers rather than being posited in someone like Isaiah or Jeremiah. Jesus is the only king in the New Testament. The doctrine of the priesthood of *all* believers finds justification in the Epistles. The imagery of the New Testament uses different terminology: stewards, shepherds, pastors, elders, deacons, and deaconesses.

The strong concept of servanthood in leadership is indicated by the use of terminology that applied to various slave functions in New Testament culture. This is significant for understanding the pastoral role. Leadership from the perspective of the servant's role would call into question many of the practices of leadership that are promoted today. These definitions of leadership are at best based on Old Testament concepts of leadership and at worst on cultural patterns of leadership in our secular communities.

There are many ways to define leadership. The model you choose will bring with it the demands of its assumptions. Hierarchical models put the pastor in a place of power, which brings with it the many stresses experienced in power relationships. A management model or coaching model involves more interpersonal skills and has danger of manipulation. A teaching-educational model assumes superior knowledge and places people in a student role who then become learners or disciples in submission to the instructor. A shepherd-pastoral model will bring a focus of nurture and care of those served.

It is not my purpose here to debate these models but to discuss the way in which the demands of ministry based upon these models may best be addressed. Different models are appropriate to different situations and the stresses change significantly from one model to another. If one begins with a more hierarchical model or a management model from a corporation perspective one will experience different issues. I would affirm that the foundational expectation of Scripture is that those called of God become servants to those they lead. The fulfillment of God's purposes in our lives leads to a life of submission to the needs of those we serve. This understanding is modified by another principle. "Each of us should please his neighbour for his good, to build him up."[86] Servanthood is not just about pleasing people. The goal is to be what others need us to be for their good that they may be built up in their faith. This requires leadership and sometimes, confrontation, not for the sake of control, rather, for achievement of Christlikeness in the believer. The demands of ministry are not for the fainthearted, the proud or those who wish acclamation. The objective for those called of God must remain the anticipation of "well done, thou good and faithful servant."[87] It is from this perspective that the following considerations are presented to enhance the endurance of those called to pastoral ministry. Integrity, community, and endurance are the great challenges in ministry today.

---

86 Romans 15:2
87 Matthew 25:21 (KJV)

An Ethic of Virtue in Ministry

This terminology requires some definition. The term *an ethic of virtue* comes from Stanley Hauerwas.[88] *Ethics* is the discipline of moral practice and *virtue* defines the practice in terms of moral excellence demonstrated in behaviour. Virtues are those qualities of behaviour that manifest morality in daily life. The pastoral role should be a demonstration of the disciplined behaviour expressed in the virtues enunciated by Paul.[89] These virtues of moral excellence provide a model for conduct in the "household of God."[90] This is a high standard that demonstrates the moral vision of the New Testament for the people of God.[91] The pastoral role should model those ethical virtues that are to characterize relationships in the church. Leadership defined in terms of these virtues provides the foundation for all of the other aspects of leadership. For this reason we should not determine our function as pastors based upon models of leadership in our culture. We would do well to demonstrate a better way by drawing our models and values from biblical understanding.

It is common in writing about leadership to focus on the valued outcomes for the church but not to focus on the ethical behaviour of pastor and people. Often, ethical behaviour is the focus only after one has fallen into unethical behaviour. There is a significant emphasis in secular literature on

---

88 S. Hauerwas, *A Community of Character* (Notre Dame, IN: University of Notre Dame, 1981) p. 113
89 1 Timothy 3:1-10 and Titus 1:5-9
90 1 Timothy 3:14
91 See Richard Hayes, *The Moral Vision of the New Testament* (San Francisco, CA: HarperCollins, 1996)

the incorporation of values and ethics into one's leadership style.[92] Often the focus is upon relational function directed toward effectiveness, success or the achievement of economic goals. Malphurs defines core values of a church and its leadership.[93] His theological perspective is of great help in applying core values to direct ministry. Goals grow out of vision and values should be at the heart of vision. We clearly need values, vision, and goals and synergy among them. However, whatever values, visions, and goals we articulate must be expressed by virtues consistent with our life in Christ.

Ethical behaviour may be expressed in professional standards of conduct. If we focused on morality and professional standards in behaviour there would be a commonality among pastors. Goals may be different among pastors but moral and professional behaviour should be common to all. Moral values and professional ethics are communal concepts, and they apply to leadership. Scripture does indicate a high standard for leadership. Christian leadership must look to God's revelation as the source of morality and ethics for its guidance. Brueggemann bluntly declares, "We owe nothing to the values of the world."[94] On the other hand, functioning in keeping with biblical standards of behaviour should exceed the values operative in the world of corporations. The tension

---

92 Three examples: Stephen R. Covey, *Principle-Centered Leadership*, (New York, NY: Fireside, Simon & Schuster , 1991); J. B. Ciulla, *Ethics: The Heart of Leadership*(West Port, CT: Praeger Publishers, 1998); Benis. & Nanus, *Leadership: The Strategies for Taking Charge*, (New York, NY: Harper & Row, 1985)

93 Aubrey Malphurs, *Value-Driven Leadership: Discovering and Developing Your Core Values for Ministry*, (Grand Rapids, MI: Baker Books, 1996).

94 W. Brueggemann, *Living Toward a Vision* (New York, NY: United Church Press, 1982) p. 116

between morality and ethics in leadership and the goals of commercial enterprise create a predicament that Christian leadership does well to avoid.[95]

Several of the professional organizations that I have associated with have ethical guidelines for their membership. This is true of the Christian Association for Psychological Studies, the Canadian Association for Pastoral Education and the Ontario Association of Consultants, Counselors, Psychometrists and Psychotherapists. At the Mental Health and Missions Conference (in 1987) a helpful presentation was provided on "Ethical Guidelines for Mental Health Professionals in Missions."[96] These articulate ethical behaviour explicitly. They illustrate what may be a lack in religious organizations and denominations. If one's denomination does not have such guidelines, it would be helpful for each pastor to clarify those ethical virtues by which he is guided. Many churches have provided such guidelines in the interest of protecting children to whom they minister. Some incorporate into those guidelines policies for the protection of volunteers who work with children. Some Christian organizations establish policies that address harassment within their organizations. All of these are helpful.

It is appropriate for pastors to pre-think these issues personally. In his behaviour in ministry, the pastor must reflect biblical concepts of godliness and holiness. Paul urged Timothy to "present himself to God as one approved, a workman who does not need to be ashamed."[97] Peterson comments on

---

95 These are discussed from a secular ethic in Ciulla, op. cit.
96 K. O'Donnell, "Ethical Principles for Mental Health Professionals in Missions" (Proceedings, MHM Conference, November, 1987).
97 1 & 2 Timothy, Titus and 1 Peter provide specific guidance to the behaviour in ministry.

holiness: "God's holiness burns the impurities, the sin, the ego from our speech so that we can speak heart to heart... Holiness no longer outside us, but inside us."[98] The best biblical model for relationships in ministry is the behaviour of Christ in his ministry. Isaiah who so frequently foresaw the coming of the Messiah wrote in anticipation, "When they see among them their children, the work of my hands, they will keep my name holy; they will acknowledge the holiness of the Holy One of Jacob, and will stand in awe of the God of Israel."[99] We are called to live lives that worship the Holy One and demonstrate his grace so that our lives may be "worthy of the calling"[100] we have received.

To breach one's virtues is to lose the integrity of heart that is so important to God. When Abraham went into the land of Gerar, he made the false assumption that "There is surely no fear of God in this place."[101] Based upon that false assumption, he introduced his wife to Abimelech as his sister. God intervened and saved Abimelech from sin, stating, "I know that you did this with a clear conscience."[102] God in visiting Solomon said, "If you walk before me in integrity of heart and uprightness...I will establish your royal throne."[103] Of Job God declared, "There is no one on earth like him; he is blameless and upright, a man who fears God and shuns evil."[104] Throughout Scripture, there is a strong emphasis upon integrity of heart.

---

98 E. Peterson, *The Jesus Way*, (Grand Rapids, MI: Eerdmans, 2007), p. 136.
99 Isaiah 29:23
100 Ephesians 4:1
101 Genesis 20:1-18
102 Genesis 20:6 (King James Version)
103 1 Kings 9:2-5
104 Job 2:3

Even in the face of such temptation, loss, abuse, and physical suffering as Job and Joseph experienced, they retained their integrity. This must be a top priority in ministry. The Hebrew word (*tom*) is translated "integrity" and "perfection." A detailed study of this word throughout the Old Testament underscores the importance of integrity in ministry and witness. In the New Testament, the requisite for bishops or elders is that they be *without reproach* or *blameless*.[105] Our goal is to be *approved of God* as well as approved of men.[106] To achieve this we must tame the lions within[107] and without[108] and avoid intellectual debate and speculation.[109] Job's integrity was tested by the loss of material possessions, family, health, wife's support, friend's support, God's presence, self-respect, and hope. Perhaps, there is no better study of the anatomy of temptation than the experience of Job and the temptation of the Lord Jesus as he began his ministry.

The retention of our integrity is a top priority. The Psalmist prays: "Guard my life and rescue me; let me not be put to shame, for I take refuge in you. May integrity and uprightness protect me, because my hope is in you." In another Psalm he pleads, "Vindicate me, O Lord, for I have led a blameless life; I have trusted in you without wavering. Test me, O Lord, and try me, examine my heart and my mind; for your love is ever before me, and I walk continually in your truth."[110] This spirit of contrition and openness to examine ourselves must be constant in our prayers and our lives. The

---

105 1 Timothy 3:2; Titus 1:6
106 Romans 16:10; 14:18; 2 Corinthians 10:18; 2 Timothy 2:15
107 1 Corinthians 9:27; 1 Timothy 4:17; 2 Timothy 2:22
108 1 Peter 5:8
109 1 Timothy 6:3ff; 2 Timothy 2:23-3:17
110 Psalm 25:20-21; Psalm 26:1-3

words *approved* and *irreproachable*, as used by Paul, speak to our pursuit of moral integrity and ethical astuteness.[111]

Having ministered to a significant number of pastors who breached their integrity, I can assure you it is very difficult to recover from such an experience.[112] Visions for ministry and the goals for their realization must be consistent with the values of Scripture but even more foundational are the behaviour and methodology by which we seek to achieve these objectives. Any loss of integrity through failure in ethical behaviour or the expression of Christian values in relationships is a showstopper for pastors. I believe in restoration to ministry following such, but it is a difficult path. Considering the enemy of our souls and the temptations on every side from our culture there may be no greater challenge in ministry than the maintenance of our integrity.

THE PASTOR'S ROLE IN CREATING COMMUNITY

The pastor's role in creating Christian community may be one of the least understood aspects of Christian ministry. It is clear from Scripture that the creation of community is an essential function of the pastor. Troubled churches are troubled communities. God chose a community of people to whom to reveal himself and through whom the nations were to come to know him. And while salvation is entered into through the

---

111 See Romans 16:10; 1 Corinthians 11:19; 2 Timothy 2:15; 1 Timothy 3:2; 5:7; 6:14

112 I would recommend reading Gordon MacDonald or D. Jeffries, *No Fall Too Far,* (Little Rock, AR: August House, 1992); D. Baker, Beyond Forgiveness (Portland, OR: Multnomah Press, 1984);R. B. Hays, (1996) op.cit.

new birth in Christ, which is a personal experience, Jesus envisaged individuals becoming a community of faith governed by different values and ethics than the culture in which they live. Terminology such as *field*, *garden*, *flock*, *body*, *family*, and *nation* are descriptors of the groups of people pastors are to nurture into maturity in Christ. Maturity primarily manifests itself in the relational rigors of community. Creating community is a must-do for pastors, for the creation of communities of faith is the goal of ministry.[113] The behaviour of these communities is what will set them apart as a witness to God's grace in human lives.

Our culture teaches us to accept ourselves as we are and to assert the personal right to be just that. But individualism impoverishes the lives of those who seek it. In our culture, the personalizing of spirituality has become the norm. The *new spirituality* is not only self-centered, it is self-defined. There is poverty in seeking the spiritual in one's *self* as its source or circumference. Neither self nor reason alone will provide the sustenance sufficient to meet the hunger of the human heart. The windows of the soul must be thrown open to the soft breeze of God's love as revealed in Christ so as to be cleansed by the sweet aroma of grace. History demonstrates conclusively that man cannot lift himself by his own bootstraps from his fallen state.

Paul states: "Christ Jesus came into the world to save sinners."[114] Not only to save them for a heavenly salvation but for an abundant life wherein his life may be demonstrated in communal living. The transformational nature of the new

---

[113] One of the helpful books that focus on the church as community is Ford, Kevin G., *Transforming Church*, (Colorado Springs, CO: David C. Cook, 2008)

[114] 1 Timothy 1:15

birth and the call to discipleship demands change, or to use Paul's word, conformity to the mind of Christ[115] expressed in the body. We are designed for community.

The Christian faith is all about a community of faith corporately committed to fulfilling the call of God; first, to change lives, and secondly, to model a transformed social entity called the body of Christ as a witness in the world. The faith community is not an option, but a necessity. Creating community is complex and brings many challenges to the pastor's role in ministry. Eugene Peterson makes an important observation in his introduction to Numbers in The Message.[116]

> Building a truly human community is a long, complex, messy business. Simply growing up as a man or woman demands all the wisdom and patience and courage that we can muster. But growing up alongside others, parents, siblings and neighbours, to say nothing of odd strangers and mean enemies, immensely complicates the process...This section of the biblical story gives us a realistic feel for what it means to be included in a human community – a community that honors God, lives out love and justice in daily affairs, learns how to deal with sin in itself and among its members and follows God's commands into a future of blessings. And all of this without illusions.

He observes, "We need organizational help" and "we need relational help" and "we need help in getting along with each

---

115 1 Corinthians 2:16

116 Peterson, Eugene (2008) "Introduction to Numbers" in *NIV/The MESSAGE Parallel Study Bible,*(Grand Rapids,MI.: Zondervan) p. 245

other. Wise discipline is required in becoming a people of God."[117] This is a great challenge for pastoral ministry but it is the essence of our role.

God called Israel to be a community of faith where his will could be evidenced as a witness to the nations. The covenant was a communal concept. The New Testament reiterates this theme via its picture of the body of Christ. Peterson says, "The lonely isolation of the solitary person must be invaded. Life, to be meaningful, must be joined: intimacy is a requirement of wholeness."[118] The place of intimacy for the believer is the community of faith. More specifically in relation to the pastor, he observes, "Pastoral conversations are conversations between persons who are seeking intimacy."[119] Believers enter a covenantal relationship with God and each other. Pulpit ministry alone cannot fulfil the pastor's responsibility.

Doubts created by liberalism in the first half of the last century contributed to the retreat of pastors from their previous role as a primary source of care in our culture. This retreat was concurrent with the rise of the pastoral psychology movement that found in psychology the hope to change people that had been lost in liberal theology. Unfortunately, many evangelical pastors followed this example and to a large extent became office practitioners. As pastoral counselling gained popularity pastors were seen less often in the marketplace of people's real lives. We must never minimize the essential role of teaching and preaching, but we must clearly direct our speaking to the creation of community by word and example. When the tapestry of God is woven to describe

---

117 Ibid

118 Peterson, Eugene ,*Five Smooth Stones for Pastoral Work* (Grand Rapids, MI: Eerdmans Edition, 1992) p. 46

119 Op. cit., p. 44

God's engagement with this generation, the threads will represent our function in our church communities.

Our opportunities to come together as a community of faith for intimacy, in concert with the Spirit of God, were largely replaced with a lecture-hall format. At the same time, pastors began to define pastoral ministry in terms of office visits rather than going into homes and workplaces to do pastoral care. Sunday worship became more like a classroom experience than an experience of intimacy in Christian community. In some cases it came to replicate entertainment or a pep rally. The experience of a community seeking intimacy with the Father, Son, and Comforter appeared to dwindle.

In discussing the communal experience of Israel in captivity, Peterson concludes, "Every church community, no matter how small, how deficient in piety, how lacking in works… is a miraculous and precious gift, an instance, no matter how obscure or flawed, of the kingdom of God, and must, for that reason, be lifted up in thanks."[120] Out of that spirit of gratitude, each pastor must begin where his community of faith is at, with all of its imperfections, so as to build a community where the members live in care and compassion for one another. Nurturing believers toward community is a primary function of the pastor. Faith is expressed in relationships.

The biblical models of community are clear in both Testaments. The calling of Israel out of slavery in Egypt and the accompanying role of Moses is an important model. The goal of Moses was to create a community faithful to Jehovah and its constituents. Nehemiah modeled community leadership as he inspired people in the face of great opposition to complete the task to which they were called. Paul created communities of faith around the Mediterranean. Walsh and

---

120 Peterson, E. (1980), op. cit. p. 214

Middleton put it rather forthrightly, "Renewal in the image of God is communal... The community is God's means of empowering people."[121] Even if a pastor does not see his giftedness or personality particularly well suited to the process of creating community, he must assume responsibility to see it happens. He will then engage others whom he can guide into that role. The creation of community cannot be left to accident. It is created intentionally and evidenced in relationships among its members as well as in its relationship to the Lord of the Church.

GOING THE DISTANCE

Everyone wishes to finish strong. Jesus explained to his disciples, "My food is to do the will of him who sent me and to finish his work."[122] We each echo the urgency with which Paul describes his ministry. He strove as an athlete, desiring to finish the course of his ministry so as to realize Christ's purpose for him.[123] He wanted to "finish the task."[124] A study of leadership and ministry in Scripture clearly indicates that leadership brings its challenges. The risks in ministry are high. Paul says, "We were harassed at every turn—conflicts on the outside, fears within."[125] Earlier in the same Epistle he said, "We are hard pressed on every side, but not crushed;

---

121 B.J. Walsh, & J. R. Middleton, Jr. *The Transforming Vision*, (Downers Grove, IN.:Inter-Varisty Press, 1984) p 160-161.
122 John 4:34
123 1 Corinthians 9:25-27; 2 Timothy 4:6-8; Philippians 3:10f
124 Acts 20:24
125 2 Corinthians 7:5

perplexed, but not in despair; persecuted, but not abandoned; struck down, but not destroyed."[126]

It is helpful to realistically acknowledge the costs and trials associated with ministry. Paul identified one of the great pressures he faced in ministry with these words, "I face daily the pressure of my concern for all the churches."[127] Remember the tensions of Moses as he led a rebellious people. Criticism, blame, competitiveness of other leaders, and outright rebellion were challenges he faced. Nehemiah's leadership was fraught with external opposition plus the internal challenge of motivating workers engaged in re-building Jerusalem's walls. Communities of faith are no different today than they were in their day. A study of the response of God's chosen leaders should be foundational to our understanding of ministry.

Crises are the crucible of the soul. They are events that demand decision. They may be a turning point. We learn from examples of individuals who prepared for anticipated crises by clarifying their commitment. Earlier, I referred to Daniel and his three friends and Jesus, who, in anticipation of a crisis, clarified their commitment in determining how they would respond before the test of demanding circumstances. Anticipation is the wisdom of seeing something before it happens and preparing a response in quietness before God. If we are to dance in the furnace, as did the three youth of Daniel's time, we also need to pre-think many issues we will encounter and prayerfully clarify our commitment as Jesus did in anticipation of the Cross. The challenge of going the distance will be different for each. We can also be assured of challenges from the enemy of souls.

---

126 2 Corinthians 4:8-9; 6:3-13; 11:23f
127 2 Corinthians 11:28

In the New Testament, Paul uses a word to express his desire to go the distance (*plerao* and *pleres*). This word is translated by a range of words: *to make full, complete, to render perfect*, and *to carry through to the end or lacking in nothing*. He states that the law is "summed up" in the single command, "Love your neighbour as yourself."[128] He speaks of "being filled with the fruit of righteousness."[129] He says, "In Christ all the fullness of the Deity dwells."[130] Then, later in that Epistle, he urges Archippus, "See to it that you complete the work you have received of the Lord."[131] The range of meaning in this word is all about completion. This is the desire of every pastor that he will complete the work of the Lord to which he has been called. Finishing strong is the desire and the intention. Among other qualities, Paul urges Timothy to pursue endurance.[132]

This is the goal all pastors could wish for when going through transitions. Transition challenges this passion. So, it is very important to deal with transition in a manner that does not lead to the sense that God has abandoned his servant. As I have listened to the heartbeat of many pastors, it is clear that they are challenged by the pain of transition to turn aside from ministry. And tragically, many do. Paul made a choice: "Forgetting what is behind and straining toward what is ahead. I press on toward the goal to win the prize for which God has called me heavenward in Christ Jesus."[133] Let us do likewise. God heals the wounds of transition. His healing can

---

128 Galatians 5:14
129 Philippians 1:11
130 Colossians 2:9
131 Colossians 4:17
132 1 Timothy 6:6-14
133 Philippians 3:13-14

strengthen the bent branches, so that they might bear fruit again. Endurance is a gift of grace that comes to those who find their solace in the God of all comfort. This resting place in God must be so secure as not to be overthrown by the storms encountered in our journey even when crossing the river of transition.

Premature Attrition and Addictions

Years of research and counselling of families in ministry, plus intense involvement with many who have experienced premature attrition has led me to see the relationship between premature attrition and addiction among those in ministry. By premature attrition, I refer to Christian leaders who terminate from ministry earlier than planned. Most often premature attrition occurs for reasons to do with health, family concerns, failure to adjust, conflicts, and the demands of ministry. Health or family concerns are deemed acceptable reasons for termination, but to oft these are cover-ups for the real reasons. These approved or permitted reasons may be proffered to explain one's leaving but frequently the real reasons for attrition or redeployment are not overtly faced. And such secondary reasons are usually provided when the primary reason is unacceptable or may bring embarrassment. Sometimes this has involved immoral behaviour, the breach of the law or of trust within an organization. When the real reasons are too painful to face or would generate too much conflict there is a tendency to obfuscate. The immediate factors that lead to removal from ministry are usually secondary to more primary issues that remain concealed.

Some of these difficulties arise within individuals while others have their origins in the organization or church itself.

Most frequently it is a combination of interpersonal factors, personal considerations and factors in the person's environment. Sometimes the toxicity present in these interactions is very great. Toxicity present in a ministry group or a congregation spreads like a virus, infecting many in the group and rendering the faith community ineffective in ministry. These may be referred to as systemic issues. Systemic issues are habitual patterns that have existed over a long enough time span as to become reactive and unconscious.

One church lost seven out of nine pastors in its history of thirty years. Different reasons were given but there were similarities. Professional assessment indicated that systemic problems in the church contributed to the failure of each pastor. These are rarely seen from within. Each pastor out of their differences of personality will engage differently. Thus, the underlying dynamic is not obvious to the people. That is not to set aside the pastor's responsibility but to recognize deeper and related issues.

Addiction is an apt word to describe the habitual behaviour of some pastors. One common addiction is over-extension, which leads to emotional fatigue. A great variety of problems come to the fore when a person becomes chronically exhausted. This occurs in ministry when pastors engage in *applauded addictions*. The cultures of many Christian organizations applaud behaviours that invariably lead to problems in the lives of pastors. Many congregations and their leadership today have increased the load on willing pastors to the point of their debilitation. Busyness, constant availability, and openness to intrusive behaviour from others are applauded. Attitudes that place expectations of 24/7 availability, the responsibility to be involved in every decision, presence at every minor crisis and limited privacy or holiday time may rob a pastor of quietness in which to seek the sustaining relationship with God that is so vital.

Such over-extension is a common addiction. It may derive from drivenness, compulsiveness, pursuit of perfection, or the expectations of a pastor. Yet, on the other hand, it can be encouraged by denominational leadership and church membership. Regardless of where it comes from this addiction to over-extension is eventually crippling. It is important to distinguish between a passionate pursuit of service to God and the soul-destroying pressure that comes from being pushed beyond one's capacity physically, emotionally, spiritually or relationally.

Both God and Jethro counselled Moses to avoid the exhaustion of over-engagement in ministry.[134] Moses was trying to do everything himself. Very often this addictive behaviour leads to depression and mood swings that are destructive of ministry. The outcome is frequently that of Elijah who became exhausted, depressed and suicidal.[135] Many things contributed to his problem including exhaustion from his battle with Baal, his fear of humans, his sense of aloneness, his hunger and just the plain physical demand of his activity. Emotional exhaustion is a very real and common outcome in ministry. It becomes very lonely when you feel you're the only one who is faithful. It is often rather difficult to personally explore one's own contribution to this condition and equally difficult to be one's own doctor in resolving the matters involved. The Scriptures are very clear about the importance of Sabbath in each of our lives. Every pastor needs to explore the helpful literature on this topic. Each person in ministry needs to know their limits. The biblical teaching concerning

---

134 Exodus 18:13-27; Numbers 11:16-17

135 1 Kings 19:3-19

Sabbath and rest requires the creation of healthy margins for renewal and recuperation.

In the third church that I pioneered, expectations drove me to depression. The mother church had experienced a fracture that led to the loss of many members and became a competing church in the city. The mother church carried on in their vision to continue the development of a daughter church in a new subdivision. It was a tense situation under pressure to succeed quickly and foster a unity between the mother and daughter church. My supervisor demanded extensive reporting. Several sermons each week, community involvement, radio broadcasts, joint services all added pressure. The desire to start a family with extremely limited financial support added to my problems. I became addicted and compulsive in responding. I provided good theological reasons for my overwork and was encouraged to "burn out for Jesus." The result was rather severe depression, discouragement, exhaustion and fatigue. Perhaps it was a need to please others, to succeed, to prove it could be done or many other factors but I was addicted. I see the situation differently as I look back over fifty years. Today, I would call it addiction. God did intervene, for which I am grateful.

The addiction of some to self-abasement may grow out of a misunderstood theological perspective expressed in terms of *death to self*. It frequently occurs along with a need to be seen as spiritual or a need to please. It may begin as an attempt to deflect praise or avoid pride or to give the impression of humility but it will eventually lead to depression or at least, a loss of joy in ministry.

Frequently, an underlying motivation behind self-abasement is the pursuit of approval. It feels so good to be liked! Affirmation is a double-edged sword. It can be very encouraging and produce positive emotions. On the other hand, to become dependent upon affirmation from others, in response to one's ministry, is ultimately self-defeating. It leads to the inability to be straightforward or confrontational. The fear of offending is crippling in ministry.

A related addiction is for warmth and love. This may manifest as wanting to be seen as the indispensable caregiver. Very frequently, this is an addiction to pleasing others, which at its root is motivated by pride. When one pursues adulation, it may be an evidence of insecurity or poor self-image. We need courage to explore our motives for pleasing others. Paul speaks of this, "We who are strong ought to bear with the failings of the weak and not to please ourselves. Each of us should please his neighbour for his good."[136] The distinction here lies between pleasing self and focusing on the good of others.

One of the most destructive things that can happen in a church or Christian organization is for the leader to fall into moral failure or indiscretion. Yet, this is a very common occurrence. Just yesterday a call from a pastor was seeking help for a brother pastor caught in the web of pornography. In my experience with leaders, moral failure most frequently occurs when some of the above addictions have been present for some time. This is true whether it manifests in sexually inappropriate behaviour, fraud, theft or other breaches of trust. Moral failure of pastors, in my experience, has always been preceded by exhaustion, or self-abasement, or the pursuit of approval and, often, depression. Understanding what led to moral failure does not relieve one of responsibility but it does help us to intervene redemptively. The path to moral failure is quite clear. In attempting to understand and to

---

[136] Romans 15:1-2

therapeutically intervene in situations where moral indiscretion has occurred, one must recognize the preceding factors.

When one is in a state of being stressed, burnt-out, depressed, lonely, or in unusual need of affirmation, that person is in great danger. Frequently, what occurs is defined as *transference* and *counter-transference*. Transference occurs when a pastor extends to a hurting person the gifts of care, compassion, comfort or consolation and the person responds by personalizing the pastoral ministry as a romantic gesture. Hurting people respond to expressed love frequently, at an unconscious level, and deeply. It feels so good to be cared for and they reciprocate with warmth, appreciation, and gratitude. They have, in essence, fallen in love with the care they have received, but these very positive feelings may be transferred to the person of the caregiver. When that happens transference has occurred. A pastor at this point is in grave danger.

If the caregiver begins to assume that the warmth and appreciation is for him as a person, rather than directed toward his caring behaviour, we have moved to counter-transference. If a pastor, in a state of exhaustion and need for approval enters into that illusion, there is a very real possibility of indiscretion taking place. The indiscretion occurs in the context of misinterpreted care and love. Pastors who misunderstand this process may bask in the warmth of that misinterpreted love and contrast it with what is experienced in their spousal relationship. It may lead to a critical appraisal of their relationship at home. The contrast between appreciation received in ministry and any perceived lack of affirmation at home provides a context for such failure.

In chapter seven, I discussed the disciples' distraction and elaborated on the competitiveness of their relationship. Addiction to competitiveness is usually justified in terms of success and finds its root in addiction to approval or success. We live in an extremely competitive culture where numerical growth, acquisition of educational degrees, largeness of churches and financial gain can quickly generate addictions for those in ministry. One does not listen long at a pastor's conference before the competitive nature of interactions becomes evident. It is easy to argue that this is celebrating what God is doing but it too frequently slips into competition or self-aggrandizement. Denominations encourage this in setting targets for growth in numbers of baptisms, church membership growth or new building enterprises. However good these goals are, in and of themselves, they may lead to feelings and actions that have destructive effects on ministry. We must each examine our lives for addiction to such competitiveness.

BURNOUT IN MINISTRY[137]

What was referred to as *battle fatigue* in the Second World War is now referred to as Post-Traumatic Stress Disorder. The symptoms are labeled as burnout or emotional exhaustion and are common among people in ministry. It is frequently an outcome of stress and trauma related to conflicts in the community of service, one's personal life experience and factors present in the personality of the pastor.

Many people in ministry evidence damaging results of stress and trauma. Stress may be seen simply as the result of

---

137 A helpful discussion of burnout from a medical, psychological and pastoral perspective is: Minirth, Hawkins, Meier and Flournoy, *How to Beat Burnout*, (Chicago, IL: Moody Press, 1986). Additional information re: Burnout may be found in: Tihab and McMinn, "Denominational Support for Clergy Mental Health, Journal of Psychology and Theology, Vol. 38, No.2, 2010, pp101-110.

constant wear and tear. Stress and trauma are evidenced physically, emotionally and spiritually where there are significant events with dire consequences. Severity of symptoms may range along a continuum of anxiety, denial, anger, depression, remorse, grief, pain, muscle tension, gastrointestinal problems, mental disorientation, confusion, and memory loss. One's sense of vulnerability increases. When a pastor begins to experience these symptoms, it is time to seek professional help. Burnout occurs when a person strains physically, emotionally or spiritually beyond God's expectation and thus, beyond grace. It is equivalent to leaping off of the temple (as the devil encouraged Jesus to do for the benefit and applause of the crowd) and constitutes a challenge to God's commitment to care for us. It may be a pursuit of vanity or pride through the received applause of man. Sometimes, it comes from a theology of self-deprivation or an inclination to asceticism. Maintaining balance between commitment to accomplish all we can for God and over-extension is a fine line and a difficult tightrope to walk. It is most helpful to assess oneself with the objectivity of identifying the symptoms and letting them speak for themselves.

If you did not do it before, let me ask you to go back to chapter four to complete the form provided: "Personal Indicators of Stress." This has been used for many years to identify the outcomes of stress in both missionaries and pastors and is a rough way to assess one's experience of stress. It is helpful to acknowledge that sources of stress include personality variables, administrative responsibilities, bureaucratic structures, work conditions, family factors, financial stress and many other contributors. The reality is that people experience stress in different ways physically, emotionally, and spiritually. It is important for each person to be aware of their typical response to stress in terms of physical, emotional, relational, and spiritual symptoms.

Differences in response are related to personality, resilience, health, social climate, family support and many other variables. Increasing one's self-awareness can be very helpful in early response and prevention. Both the sources of stress and the responses to stress are personal and the changes associated with transition are very stressful. Change that impacts family, spouse, children, friends or fellow workers will induce stress. Perfectionism, neuroticism, limited tolerance for ambiguity, difficulty with anger management and many other personal variables will create stress. The next chapter will identify resources for preventing, coping an ameliorating stress.

> The fruit of righteousness will be peace;
> the effect of righteousness will be quietness and confidence forever.
> My people will live in peaceful dwelling places,
> in secure homes, in undisturbed places of rest.
>
> Isaiah 32:17-18

Questions for Reflection

How would I define my values and ethics as they express themselves in my leadership role? Do I have these in writing for frequent review? How am I fulfilling God's expectation that I create a community of faith that manifests Christian relationships? How would I describe my desire to finish strong? Are there behaviours that I could describe as addictive in my approach to ministry? What are the areas in which I see evidence of stress in my life?

Chapter Nine

The Care & Maintenance of Pastors

> Moses's father-in-law replied, "What you are doing is not good. You and these people who come to you will only wear yourselves out."
>
> Exodus 18:17

> Guard the good deposit that was entrusted to you—guard it with the help of the Holy Spirit who lives in us.
>
> 2 Timothy 1:14

> The elders who direct the affairs of the church well are worthy of double honour, especially those whose work is preaching and teaching.
>
> 1 Timothy 5:17

Since transition is a major and sometimes frequent experience for those engaged in ministry it is wise to explore the different options for effective care to assist pastors in this common experience. One can prepare for and can open oneself for the assistance of others in crossing the river of transition. Needs will vary from one situation to another and understanding the process is extremely important. It is critical to individualize the experience to achieve an understanding of what is involved for each person. The response must be tailored to the needs of each pastor and church. Many of the interventions suggested will assist in responding to this helpfully.

Transition should be placed in the context of the larger issue of the care and nurture of pastors along their career path. Most often, the care and nurture of pastors is very inadequately addressed. Many pastors are reluctant to acknowledge their pain and churches appear not to be aware of this important consideration. Care involves much more than intervention at the time of crisis.

Preventive measures are more effective than crisis management and will often forestall the trauma of transition. Forestalling trauma is more efficient than intervention and reflects the passion of God for those who serve him. Continuous and ongoing care prevents the accumulation of stress just as physical well-being is best built on a foundation of good nutrition, physical exercise and good social habits. Spiritual, emotional, and social well-being is a basic need. Well-being in ministry is dependent upon foundational issues that must be constantly addressed and nurtured if we are to experience the fullest possible potential in ministry.

The care and maintenance of pastors is crucial to the well-being of churches. To neglect this responsibility is to create ineffective churches that plateau at a level of that destroys the very witness we are to have in our communities. The well-being of pastors and churches is synergistic in nature. The one is dependent upon the other.

THE CARE OF BIBLICAL LEADERS

Care is commended in Scripture for those in leadership. A study of Moses's life will readily show the need of care for leaders. It was only the nurture that he received in his encounters with God on the mountain that sustained his ministry to the chosen people of God. His partnership with Aaron and Miriam was supportive at times. Sharing one's ministry with close associates greatly contributes to endurance and care. Jethro, the priest of Midian, heard all that God had done for Moses and the people of Israel. He came and celebrated "all the good things the Lord had done for Israel"[138] and praised the Lord. However, when he saw the pattern of overextension in Moses's ministry, he assumed the role of a mentor and led Moses in sharing the load with capable men who feared God.[139] Many pastors have not learned to share their ministry and some burn out by standing alone. They experience the fate of Elijah who thought that he alone was faithful and capable.[140] God ministered to him with compassion and provided a companion and successor in Elisha. A rebellious and angry Jonah was confronted by a gracious God who wished to be known for his forgiving spirit. Another model of an encouraging leader in the Old Testament is Nehemiah, who nurtured those who worked with him.

The church in the New Testament provides examples of the reciprocal nurture of church leaders and itinerant church planters. Paul was constant in nurturing the pastors in local churches; through his writing and his visits he affirmed them with gratitude and promoted their care. With great love, he instructed churches as to the care and response they should show to their elders and pastors. Paul urged churches to honour their leaders and nurture them.[141] Paul is definitive about the need to eliminate traces of competitiveness or its

---

138 Exodus 18:1
139 See Exodus 18
140 1 Kings 19
141 Philippians 2:29;1 Timothy 5:17 and 1 Thessalonians 5:13

promulgation among leaders in 1 Corinthians. The epistles of Paul to Timothy and Titus evidence his concern to nurture and care for them in ministry. His affirmation of his coworkers at the end of most of his letters evidences even more so his care for fellow workers. And, he was very careful to nurture the leadership at Ephesus as he was on his way to Jerusalem.[142] But Paul also received care, and that, with great gratitude, from Titus when the pressure of ministry became stressful for him in Macedonia.[143]

One of Peter's responsibilities was to "strengthen your brothers" after he was restored to ministry.[144] Jesus cared for his disciples in pre-ministry preparation and post-ministry debriefing as he sent them from village to village.[145] He prayed for Peter in anticipation of his failure and later renewed him to ministry. The last discourse of Jesus (John 14-17) clearly expresses his love and care for his disciples. He promised the coming of the Holy Spirit who was to be a constant companion in their lives and ministry.

As implied earlier, the Epistles clearly demonstrate the care that the churches had for their leaders and the passion of Paul to nurture his fellow workers. Christians are urged to give to their leadership all due respect and honour in providing for their needs and sustaining them in ministry. Both denominations and churches need to have practical policies in place that provide recuperation, renewal and intervention for their pastors. Prevention should be paramount. Pastors who burn out or become traumatized in ministry invariably have had no sabbatical or provision for funding for their care.

---

142 Acts 20:13-36
143 2 Corinthians 7:5-7
144 Luke 22:32
145 Matthew 10; Mark 6:6ff; and Luke 10:1-20

This book has focused on the trauma of transition, but if adequate care were provided transitions would not be so traumatic. There would still be pain around some dimensions of transition (such as loss and change) but much of the stress could be removed if care were provided during the days of ministry. The absence of such care is very frequently the cause of premature attrition.

The Dimensions of Care

There are several perspectives from which care should be defined:

- Divine Care
- Self-Care
- Family Care
- Peer Care
- A Spiritual Care Group
- Denominational Care
- Church Care
- Professional Care

In other writings, I have discussed the provision of continual care for missionaries along their career path from the perspective of theology, mental health and personal responsibility.[146] The care of pastors has some similarities and some differences.

When we purchase a car, we are wise to have a plan for its care and maintenance. Care is a constant that demands

---

[146] In Powell and Bowers (eds.), *Enhancing Missionary Vitality* (Colorado Springs: Mission Training International, 2002) chapters 7,9,25.

cleanliness and appropriate usage. Maintenance includes such things as oil changes, lubrication, checking the cooling system and other aspects of a car's functioning, on a schedule designed to make the vehicle last over the long haul. Maintenance and care are intensified when usage is heavy or the conditions are extreme. Sometimes when we don't care for things they become broken or damaged beyond repair. Then, we often discard them and look for something new. Organizations understand that maintaining the well-being of their employees leads to longevity and effectiveness. The bottom line is impacted positively by good personnel policies that sustain their work force.

One organization engaged in high stress ministry to street youth found that over-committed and highly dedicated staff needed special attention and supervision. Street workers were being lost through burnout and discouragement. A policy was put in place that limited workers to a fifty hour week requiring that when this limit was reached they take time off. Secondly, a key person was assigned to provide pastoral care for the youth who had made professions of faith so that the street workers were freed to focus on their street evangelism. The result was that the best and most committed workers ceased to be in jeopardy. Sometimes compassion leads to over-extension and premature attrition. Provision of care for these street workers, plus appropriate limitations on their overload solved the problem.

The life expectancy of pastors in ministry is very different than maintaining autos or organizations. However, they just as assuredly require care on a daily basis and regular maintenance checks. If not cared for they wear out before their time or become broken and are discarded. Some pastors have expressed the feeling of being a *throwaway* item that is discarded whenever church leadership feels there should be a change.

Both George and Sam felt discarded by church leadership and were given no recourse to clarify the reason for their dismissal or an opportunity to respond to any complaints.[147] George was simply informed that someone (who remained anonymous for sake of confidentiality) had complained. The leadership took the complaint seriously and asked for George's resignation. Sam was dismissed without clarification of cause at the apparent whim of a senior pastor who had the support of the leadership team. These experiences are not isolated incidents. I am not so naïve as to be unaware that there are two sides to such stories. However, in these situations there was no openness to hear the perspective of the pastors or to communicate openly and honestly. The absence of honest communication inhibits growth and increases discouragement and loss of confidence in one's giftedness. Often replacing personnel appears to be considered an easier road than that of providing care, compassion or redemptive retraining.

The care of pastors must be planned to be continuous over the entire career path. Each church shares that responsibility for the time that a pastor participates in its ministry. The denomination's concern should extend over the entire lifetime of pastors. The responsibility does not solely lie with the church or the denomination; many other sources of care are available and need to be utilized for their contribution to endurance and effectiveness. What follows is a brief presentation of the eight dimensions of care suggested above.[148]

---

147 See stories one and three in chapter one.

148 Additional information may be found in three chapters which summarized presentation I provided at a Mental Health and Missions Conference. Powell and Bowers, op.cit.: Three chapters by Glenn C. Taylor.

THE CARING GOD

In the Old Testament it is abundantly clear that God enters into a relationship in which he can care for those he calls to serve him. God met with Adam and Eve in Eden, desiring the relationship he had designed for them. Abraham was called the "friend of God"[149] and having called him, God sustained him in every situation. The constancy of God's care and communication with Moses was evidenced from his call to his death.

The intimacy of God's relationship with Moses runs throughout Exodus 24-34. Moses and his associates were summoned to "come up to the Lord." However, "Moses alone is to approach the Lord." Later after being in the presence of the Lord, Moses "went and told the people all the Lord's words and laws." After much instruction God gave Moses the Decalogue. In chapter 33 and 34, we have an excellent model of the relationship between the Lord and Moses. In the face of God's anger over the golden calf, Moses intercedes with the Lord. The degree of openness, freedom, and intimacy in this relationship is to be sought and found by each pastor. God and Moses both expressed their anger. They negotiated in an interactive way such that each could understand the passion of the other. Moses shared his frustration in ministry (33:12-23) and received the promise, "My presence will go with you, and I will give you rest ... I will do the very thing you have asked, because I am pleased with you and I know you by name." Moses pleaded, "Now show me your glory." The closeness, comfort, and enabling that we see in this relationship is what each pastor needs to sustain his continuance in ministry.

When Paul was placed in a barracks by a Roman commander, we read, "The following night the Lord stood near

---

149 2 Chronicles 20:7; James 2:23

Paul and said, 'Take courage! As you testified about me in Jerusalem, so you must also testify in Rome.'"[150] And, in the midst of shipwreck on the way to Rome, Paul addressed the crew, "Last night an angel of the God whose I am and whom I serve stood beside me."[151] Paul appears to have had the same degree of intimacy with God as did Moses. One could reference many leaders whom God called and constantly enabled and nurtured intimately. Personally, I return to the call of Isaiah and Jeremiah for affirmation of God's care. Isaiah reminds me that I come as a sinful man in need of redemption but in responding to God's call, I am commissioned. As a teenager, when God called me, I was so aware of my youth and inadequacy that I found, and continue to find, encouragement in Jeremiah's call. During sixty years of ministry I have often felt Jeremiah's sentiment: "I am only a child."[152] We need the constancy of God's touch and promise to Jeremiah. "The Lord reached out his hand and touched my mouth and said to me, 'Now, I have put my words in your mouth. See, today I appoint you ... I am with you and will rescue you.'"[153]

Jesus was very clear in his discourse following the last supper with the disciples about his compassion, care and concern for them in their ministry.[154] They had very little understanding of what lay before them. He called them friends; chosen to bear fruit and assured them he would send another Counsellor, the Holy Spirit, to meet their need for a counsellor and guide. The endurance of a pastor depends much upon his relationship with God. The prayer of Jesus for his dis-

---

150   Acts 23:11
151   Acts 17:23
152   Jeremiah 1:6
153   Jeremiah 1:9-10,19
154   John 14-17

ciples and for us is a source of constant comfort. The desire of God for a sustaining relationship with those who serve him is indubitable. Such a relationship is so vital that each must find this personal experience of a deep relationship with God if they are to be at all successful in ministry.

There are many ways to fill our minds with faith. Paul, speaking of Abraham writes that he "was strengthened in his faith and gave glory to God."[155] The word *strengthened* could be translated *empowered*. In ministry we must be empowered by faith. The disciplines of the Christian life that have proven so helpful to all generations are a good place to start. Our journey with God is very personal, but it is helpful to identify principles others have discovered in entering into a love-filled and sustaining relationship with God. This is the foundation we all seek. No doubt, each must find his own individual menu for the nourishment needed to sustain their relationship with the Lord. We should not be critical of each other's menu, but personalize our own search so as to identify what leads us into God's sustaining grace. I can share with you one of the passages of Scripture that I like to keep constantly before me in a personally prepared format.

You have been raised with Christ—Set your hearts on things above -Set your minds on things above

You have died, and your life is now hidden with Christ in God

When Christ, who is your life, appears—You will appear with him in glory.

---

155 Romans 4:20

Put to death, therefore, whatever belongs to your earthly nature—Sexual immorality, impurity, lust, evil desires, and greed

The Wrath of God is coming—You used to walk in these ways, in the life you once lived.

BUT NOW, you must rid yourselves of all such things—anger, rage, malice, slander and filthy language from your lips—Do not lie to each other since you have taken off your old self with its practices.

And have put on the new self—which is being renewed in knowledge in the image of its Creator—here there is no Greek or Jew, circumcised or uncircumcised, barbarian, Scythian, slave or free

Christ is all, and is in all.

Therefore as God's chosen people—holy and dearly beloved

Clothe yourselves with—compassion, kindness, humility, gentleness, and patience—Bear with each other and forgive whatever grievances you may have against one another

Forgive as the Lord forgave you

Over all these virtues put on *love*—which binds them all together in perfect unity.

Let the *peace* of Christ rule in your hearts—since as members of one body you were called to peace

Be thankful

> **Let the word of Christ dwell in you richly**—as you teach and admonish one another with all wisdom—as you sing psalms, hymns, and spiritual songs **with gratitude in your hearts to God. And whatever you do, whether in word or deed, do it all in the name of the Lord Jesus, Giving thanks to God the Father through him.** [156]

Our covenantal relationship with God is our sustenance. The nurture that comes from the vine sustains the branch. Our energizing and enabling is sustained as we walk with him in a personalized way. I would suggest that God refreshes us in a manner consistent with our stage in life. He responds to us where we are in life. There is no one way. At one point in life Scripture memorization may be what helps us along. At another time, quietness in restful contemplation and prayer will strengthen the weary. Sometimes with a quiet voice and sometimes with a voice of thunder, God speaks and we are nourished. He responds to a hungry heart.

My Responsibility

Each person has a responsibility to provide for the care of self. Recently, a pastor said, "I was taught we were to burn out for God rather than rust out!" These are not the only two options! This pastor had in fact *burnt out* as a result of a very successful and affirmed ministry. He lived thirty-five years of ministry in eighteen and was now paying the price. Over-investment brings a very high cost in the long run, and the cost for him was exhaustion, depression, ill-defined

---

156 Colossians 3:1-17

physical discomfort, and a weariness that was incapacitating. Compassion-fatigue that comes from excessive stretching of reserves leaves one running on empty. God is more efficient in his call to us. He desires our service over the long haul. He knows our capacity and energizes us by the Spirit to do his will. When we reach beyond his enabling we become self-dependent with destructive consequences. Others may encourage us to over-extend, but I believe God desires us to function within the enablement that he provides.

We need to covenant with ourselves in spiritual, physical, emotional, relational, and moral commitments that will sustain us through the rigors of ministry. Furthermore, most pastors do not care for themselves physically. Eliminating the stress of normal ministry requires physical exercise to keep burnout in remission. Activity that involves cardio-vascular, stretching, and strengthening exercises is foundational.

One of the most difficult emotions that pastors deal with is anger. The incapacitating anger that Moses, Elijah, and Jonah experienced was an outcome of the stress from excessive demands of ministry, fear of opposition or dissatisfaction with God. Much anger that is experienced in ministry arises from a breach of one's values, expectations, sense of self-worth and the blocking of one's goals. Most people do not express anger well. Patterns of expression are formed early in life, and these become the default position when anger is aroused. Addressing the source of anger with more effective and appropriate responses offers a better path to resolution.[157]

Self-care requires that we understand our emotional responses and develop appropriate and disciplined ways of

---

[157] This is discussed in more detail in books co-authored with Dr. Rod Wilson. Taylor and Wilson, *Helping Angry People* and *Exploring Your Anger* (Grand Rapids.: Baker, 1997 and Vancouver: Regent, 2003).

expression. It is not enough to practise discipline if that entails suppression. We need transformation that leads to different behavioural responses rather than explosive or implosive behaviour. We would benefit from exploring alternative ways to express our emotional responses even when these feelings are justified. Our emotional responses are a gift from God and engage physiology, mind, will, and heart. The gifts of the Holy Spirit, the behaviour of love, and the qualities that are required of leadership all speak to our emotional experience and expression. As discussed earlier, moral failure in ministry develops in contexts of stress, inadequate awareness of, and inappropriate meeting of emotional needs in the lives of pastors. Emotional needs are different for each of us. Emotional needs are met through hobbies, music, play, reading for pleasure, art, outdoor activity, and a myriad of other means peculiar to each of us as individuals. These are not options, but necessities if we desire longevity in ministry. Spiritually, physically, emotionally, and socially healthy pastors survive the traumas of transition and move toward creating healthy communities of faith. Our next section will deal with emotional needs as they are met relationally.

Family, the Place of Comfort

A large percentage of pastors are married. The marriage relationship and the family are two of the most powerful influencers toward effective, sustained ministry. Frequently, a significant contributing factor to stress in ministry, especially in times of transition, arises within the family relationships. On the other hand, the most helpful contributors to the survival of transition are one's spouse and family. These relationships may be either sustaining or a source of stress. Why do we have these two extremes?

There are several factors that can be identified. One's spousal relationship is impacted by ministry, by a sense of mutual engagement in ministry, by reciprocal affirmation of respective roles, by the church's expectations of the wife's engagement in ministry and the degree of defensiveness and its expression. Each spouse will be defensive of the other. If both spouses equally experience the call to ministry, the potential for endurance increases. The powerful emphasis on individuality in our culture has permeated the spousal relationship in many cases. The wife who says, "My calling is to fulfill my gifts in my life" or, the husband who explores a church call in terms of his own personal decision is evidencing little mutuality of call. The biblical emphasis on spouses being *one* has serious implications for one's call.

Let me illustrate. Many years ago a very successful medical doctor and his wife were referred to me. Bill was a compassionate Christian and a very successful doctor. A college friend had gone to the mission field in medical ministry. Understanding the excessive workload and his friend's need for respite, Bill decided to volunteer to relieve his friend for a couple of months. He purchased a new car for his wife and, in giving her the keys, informed her of his plan to volunteer for this project without prior consultation with her. On return from his two-month stint, he expressed a sense of God's call to serve overseas. His wife's response was, "I married a doctor not a missionary! I cannot leave family and friends!" Sadly, the issue was never resolved, and the marriage dissolved. This happens with some frequency among pastors. There is a principle for us to deduce from this illustration.

When requested to provide counsel and consultation for the mission/church community in East Africa in 1975, I indicated the desire to take my wife with me. The added expense was an obstacle to which some objected. I expressed the principle I learned from the illustration above: "I should not expose myself to what could be a life-changing event without my wife being a part of it." The call of God to one spouse, if personalized and individualized, can create tensions that inhibit the fulfillment of the call of both. My recommendation to pastors is that they take their spouse to the early discussions when considering a new ministry. If God has called us together as a couple in the *oneness of marriage*, he will call us in *oneness* to ministry. Personally, I would extend that principle further by affirming that my wife is one with me in ministry, and it is not possible to have one of us without the other. This may create an issue for those who object to women in ministry, but I believe the oneness of the spousal relationship is a more foundational principle. The personalizing of a pastor's call is sometimes justified by the concept of headship in the Scripture. An equally powerful biblical doctrine is the oneness that is to be realized in the marriage relationship. Partners who function in oneness will experience oneness in call. Oneness is a biblical concept that does not abuse the integrity, honour or individuality of either spouse.

If called as a couple to be united in marriage, it follows that there is mutuality in ministry. The ministry that I experienced in Africa and other places in the world was as much my wife's ministry as it was mine. Indeed, it is not an exaggeration to say that my ministry would not have been possible without my wife as a partner in ministry. The ministry of a married couple is an expression of God's grace through their union; we divide what is indivisible from God's perspective at our peril.

The key factor in a marriage relationship is reciprocal affirmation and strengthening, out of which the two express their giftedness of God's grace. Truly, we are in this together with our spouses. As such, we need to resist the cultural pressure to individualism, women's liberation, self-actualization and many other facets of our culture that mitigate against God's institution of marriage.

The pressure that some wives feel placed upon them by the expectations of a church should be addressed early in any discussion with a prospective place of ministry. It is expected that the wife of a pastor will be engaged and may minister out of her giftedness. However, the stereotype placed by some churches on the wife is inappropriate. A wife's involvement must consider all the factors such as children, the need for additional income, the giftedness and health of the wife. Let me share a conversation that occurred early in the ministry of William and Sally as they entered a new church experience. This illustration of a real conversation makes a significant point.

> Norma (leader of a Bible study group): "Sally, would you speak at our study Group?"
>
> Sally: "Thank you, but I don't do public speaking."
>
> Norma: "But, you are a pastor's wife, aren't you?"
>
> Sally: "Yes, but tell me, what does your husband do?!"
>
> Norma: "He is a dentist."
>
> Sally: "Then, do you pull teeth and can I come to you for dental work?"

The spouse of a pastor must prioritize her responsibilities to her husband, her family, other responsibilities, and the need to be intimately involved in a community of faith. It is wisdom to clarify these expectations when negotiating a call to ministry.

Especially in times of stress and transition, the natural defensiveness of a spouse for her husband may come into play. Confidentiality often requires that not all information be shared with a spouse; this has nothing to do with trust but frees the wife to relate without prejudice. There is no sense in unnecessarily burdening one's wife with church problems that can inappropriately occupy the time a pastor must have for his family. However, when a pastor is criticized or mistreated it is normal for a wife to become defensive. Such feelings are appropriate, but need to be carefully processed before being expressed.

The pastor's marriage and his relationship with his children can provide for him one of the greatest resources of care and maintenance. A research group in which I participated explored the experience of several hundred families in ministry overseas.[158] A very close link was observed between spiritual life, satisfaction in ministry, spiritual disciplines and family life variables including marriage satisfaction. Careful thought and planning can maximize the potential of one's family to greatly enhance one's potential in ministry.

WHAT ARE FRIENDS FOR?

Ministry is not for lone rangers. The strong, stand-alone individual is not the picture of ministry that we find in the Scripture or in church history. The fictional characters that are presented as singly having conquered great obstacles in

---

[158] These results were reported in peer review journal articles and in Andrews, L.A., ed., *The Family in Missions: Understanding and Caring for those Who Serve* (Colorado Springs, CO.: Mission Training International, 2004)

ministry for God better represent the heroes of the American dream than they represent reality. Sometimes like Don Quixote, who read too many chivalric novels and dashed off tilting windmills and chasing the *impossible dream*, pastors shape their dreams around the strong imaginary and solitary figure, which is more shaped by fiction than the lives of real people. Most individuals who accomplished much for God did so with the support, camaraderie, and strengthening from those who stood with them. Paul is good example. He was not the strong loner. In fact, when left alone in Athens and Corinth he became discouraged. Strong leader that he was, he needed the fellow workers on whom he depended for affirmation and comfort in his ministry. When Paul came to Troas he says, I "had no peace of mind, because I did not find my brother Titus there." Later he said, "When we came into Macedonia, this body of ours had no rest, but we were harassed at every turn—conflicts on the outside, fears within. But God, who comforts the downcast, comforted us by the coming of Titus."[159] Every pastor needs a buddy.

We never ventured out without a buddy when scuba diving. On one occasion while diving at thirty-five feet in Gulf of Mexico, I ran out of air. I hand signalled my situation to my buddy who responded by sharing his mouthpiece and oxygen with me as we surfaced. Without my buddy present I would not have surfaced alive. What a demonstration of instant resuscitation; he enabled me to breathe again! This illustrates peer commitment; it illustrates the coming alongside that is to characterize believers in the way Titus did with Paul. It is of great importance for pastors to find in their communities or among their fellow pastors a place of hospitality and rest where they can unburden in confidence and experience

---

159 2 Corinthians 2:12-13; 7:5-6

the nurture of fellow-strugglers. It appears to me that pastors who survive do so not simply by the strength of their relationship with the Lord but also by the strength of their bonding with others who will stand with them.

Frequently, younger pastors who are called to serve on a multiple-staff team suffer loneliness and despair because nurture is not a part of the vision of the team members. The focus of team meetings is more frequently on the activity of ministry and motivation for ministry, rather than the personal lives of those who minister. Team care is modelled among the leaders in the New Testament, especially Barnabus and Paul, and by Moses, Nehemiah, and Gideon in the Old Testament.

A Spiritual Care Group

A ministry option that has proven very helpful is a spiritual care group designed for pastors who may require support, consultation or encouragement. This approach can have broad application from general care to providing care in specific situations. The degree of formality will depend largely upon the circumstances being addressed. Some pastors in the association meetings with other pastors receive care, nurture, affirmation, and clarification of ministry concerns.

The care that pastors may provide for one another can be as formal or informal as is desired. Some define their relationship in terms of accountability. They may agree to accountability questions that may be as personal or general as is helpful to their purpose. It is advisable to determine the degree of intimacy expected at the beginning and to let that grow naturally as mutual trust increases.

The formation of a more formal Spiritual Care Group (SCG) that offers mentoring, partnership and caring for pastors in transition has demonstrated favourable results. Some churches have been encouraged to create a SCG by inviting three pastors to serve a fellow pastor in transition by meeting bi-monthly for a significant period of time for support. This more formal approach will often be appropriate if the separation of pastor and church has been involuntary or unpredictably fractured as in the case of moral failure or conflict. If there is significant hurt, emotional upheaval or anger present, the creation of a Spiritual Care Group can be of great assistance.

A SCG may be created by a church, by the denomination, or by a pastor on his own behalf. When a ministry is terminated because of moral failure or the result of some trauma, the SCG should be brought into existence as early possible. The intention of this group is to facilitate the pastor's exploration of the issues that caused his termination in safety and confidentiality. There can be differences in the objectives, depending upon whether the pastor has chosen to leave or has been required to leave. It is rarely possible or desirable for a church that has terminated a pastor to continue to be involved. It is more appropriate for them, as an expression of their care for the well-being of the pastor, to transfer responsibility for care to SCG. Usually, whether the offer of a SCG is made by the church or denomination, the pastor must participate voluntarily.

If the offer is accepted, the confidentiality of the SCG is crucial. The church or denomination may wish to know if the pastor has accepted the offer but should leave the SCG to do its ministry unencumbered by any expectation of reporting. My expectation is that the SCG be a volunteer service but if travel is involved, the church or denomination may wish to cover those expenses. The purpose of the group must be clearly defined upfront. The intention is to address needs for repentance, confession, spiritual restoration, and relational problems. It is best to start with one's personal relationship with the Lord, spouse, and family before dealing with any issues related to a restoration of relationship with the church. The biblical mandates of confrontation, comfort, edification, and encouragement will direct the ministry of the group. It has been my practice in serving pastors in this way to require specific reading that deals with the issues involved. This must be more than a *feel good* experience and must deal with the tough spiritual issues. Grounding the work of the SCG in a proper theological framework is essential. The care and nurture of pastors is the responsibility of both denominational leadership and churches. It would be wise for a denomination to have a list of experienced pastors with appropriate giftedness to serve in SCG groups that they would offer to pastors or churches. It is helpful to have a brief manual to guide SCGs in forming and implementing their ministry to pastors.

Denominational Care

Some denominations have bishops or other designated providers of care who supervise pastors in their churches. However, there are many denominations that provide little support for their pastors. Many pastors report that conferences arranged by denominations focus more upon the equivalent of a *pep rally* or motivational sales meeting where, as mentioned earlier, they are pushed to achieve more. They often complain that the guest speakers create expectations and engender guilt that they find depressing. Another complaint often heard is the competitive nature of pastoral conversations that compare numerical success. The goals of care are more effectively accomplished in smaller groups where the potential for vulnerability and confidentiality is increased.

Denominations could provide a list of referral possibilities of people trained in both counselling and theology. Certainly, there should be a fund to assist pastors who need financial assistance to receive the care they need. There is great potential in retired pastors to provide support to younger men. This option would require some encouragement and, perhaps, facilitating on the part of denominations or associations. It would be helpful to create guidelines to clarify the expectations of such a relationship. These can be viewed as coaching, mentoring or spiritual guidance. Much encouragement of these relationships needs to come from denominational leadership. Many of these possibilities cannot exist without willingness on the part of pastors to open themselves to such involvement. The skills required to provide a hospitable environment for such support would be necessary for the relationship to be effective.

A Caring Community

Churches may not have a clear understanding of their responsibility to care for pastors, or how that might be done. Many pastors are uncomfortable in providing this information to churches. It would be helpful for churches to be informed by denominational leadership how a healthy pastor-church relationship could be maintained. Leadership in churches is not adequately informed of this dimension of their responsibility. The boundaries between pastor and church leadership seem to be rarely articulated. Few churches have a policy of continuing education, sabbatical periods or the provision for response to health needs that go beyond the normal health insurance.

Many pastors are not provided for adequately in terms of financial needs, ongoing need for books and electronic facility for sermon preparation. It is particularly stressful for pastors in our current economy to acquire the resources to purchase a home without additional help from their church. The biblical emphasis on *respect* and *honour* that is due the servant of God is not a topic most pastors are comfortable to preach about. Both the abuse of pastors and the failure to honour them is identified in recent research as a primary cause of church ineffectiveness.[160] Some laymen aspire to fulfill their leadership ambitions through church offices and can be very difficult for pastors to deal with. Church leadership has a responsibility to create an environment in which a pastor can fully express his ministry in meeting the needs of the church community. This message to church leadership must frequently come from denominational input such as a training program for church leaders.

The Role for the Professional

It appears in some quarters there is a stigma attached to the notion of pastors needing professional help. Some attribute such needs to a lack of spirituality. Each pastor would do well to come to grips with the reality that at some point in their ministry they will benefit from medical, psychiatric, psychological or outside pastoral services of a professional nature. Much pain in a pastor's life can be forestalled if these services are accepted, especially when it would forestall the need for much more extensive care. The object of care and

---

160 Cannon, George (2011) "A Descriptive Study of the Additional Factors Needed to Transition a Troubled Church to Health." Doctoral thesis http://digitalcommons.liberty.edu/doctoral/393.

maintenance is to glorify God by enabling endurance and effectiveness in ministry.

Each of the individuals or groups discussed above can contribute. However, it must begin with the willingness of a pastor to become sufficiently vulnerable as to enter into the experience. Paul urged Timothy, "Guard what has been entrusted to your care."[161] This was in the context of charging him to fulfill the ministry that Paul elsewhere describes as a trust. To Archippas Paul challenges: "See to it that you complete the work you have received in the Lord."[162] This is the goal we seek, the completion of the work that God has entrusted to us for his glory.

> Here is your God! See, the Sovereign Lord comes with power,
> and his arm rules for him. See, his reward is with him,
> He tends his flock like a shepherd…Those who hope in the Lord shall renew their strength.
>
> Isaiah 40: 9-11, 31

Questions for Reflection

To what extent am I willing to acknowledge the benefit or need for my own personal care and nurture? What might inhibit a pastor's willingness to accept such input? Define areas of accountability that would be helpful to include in guidelines for peer, family, church, or spiritual care group opportunities. How could concerns about confidentiality or privacy be assured?

---

161 1 Timothy 6:11-21
162 Colossians 4:17

Chapter Ten

A Biblical Account of Commitment, Failure, and Restoration

> Not only that—count yourselves blessed every time people put you down…My prophets and witnesses have always gotten into this kind of trouble.
>
> Beatitudes (MSG)

I wish now to look at the experience of Jesus's disciples and of Peter in particular from the perspective of transition. These men transitioned from being fishermen to being followers of Jesus. Each person called to ministry experiences such transition. It may be transition from tentative discipleship to being a committed follower or to a life vocation centered on ministry. Perhaps Jesus's disciples responded out of curiosity, wonder or some unrecognized movement of God's Spirit within. There was a progression involved. Their lives had stability as fishermen with all the predictability, fulfillment in known tasks, employment in practised skills, and a steady income. Then, Jesus invited them into an adventure with unknown risks they could never have imagined. They would come to experience opposition, self-doubt, and demand from others and a call for faith in their leader of a quality different to anything they could ever have dreamed. It was to be a life of risk and uncertainty. Their experience was much like that of many who are called today.

We can only imagine what prompted them to respond as they did. What did they expect the outcome to be of such a call into such a vast unknown? In response to the question from two of them about his residence, Jesus said, "Come and you will see."[163] As he gathered his disciples, they were at first only observers, later to become followers, witnessing his ministry and hearing his teaching. Later, after a night of prayer, Jesus called twelve from among many disciples to be his apostles.[164] By this time they had witnessed significant opposition from the Pharisees and had begun to understand some of the cost of following Jesus. They experienced many bumps along the way. Their every commitment to this new Galilean leader was called into question by the trauma of immediate opposition, by the testing of their faith, and by the bitter taste of failure in ministry.[165] It must have been difficult for them to deal with the ambiguity of their situation amid the ebb and flow of acceptance and rejection that they witnessed in the responses of the people to Jesus. They experienced frequent challenges to their commitment and suffered much confusion about what they became engaged in. They even became competitive with each other for pre-eminence in their own small group.[166]

The extreme trauma of Jesus's arrest and crucifixion sent them into a tailspin. Recommitment and recommissioning by Jesus and their forced dispersal because of opposition eventually ejected them from their homes to be dispersed throughout the known world. We would benefit from understanding that

---

163 John 1:37-39
164 Luke 6:12-16
165 Matthew 17:14-22
166 Mark 9:33-36

we follow in the footsteps of generations who came after the apostles, experienced similar ambiguity and had similar experiences in ministry. The transitions from one ministry to another today present us with many similar challenges to our faith.

One of the most meaningful stories in the Bible, for pastors in ministry, is the story of Peter. We are given more detail about Peter's experience than about any other disciple; maybe he is in some way representative of them all. Yet, on the other hand, he was unique in his forwardness and expressiveness. His is a story of a disciple who chose to follow, who committed himself and his future to the Lordship of Christ, who openly declared his faith and loyalty, and who in a most troubling hour experienced failure and sorrow. Then, when he met the *resurrected* Savior, he was recommissioned to ministry and continued loyal to the end, finishing strong. Let me remind you of the sequence of his life's events in relation to the Lord. Though our experiences are different, we can readily identify with all the changing emotions that this man endured.

THE CALL

The brief biblical record indicates that each one called by Jesus was summoned in a different way. Peter will provide our example as one who responded and followed.

The day after his baptism, Jesus was declared to be the Lamb of God by John the Baptist. Andrew, having heard John's remarks, followed Jesus. Andrew went to find his brother Simon and said, "We have found the Messiah." Then, Andrew brought him to Jesus, who on seeing Simon said, "You are Simon son of John. You will be called Cephas (which, when translated, is Peter)." Thus, a relationship began. A little later we read: "As Jesus was walking beside the

Sea of Galilee, he saw two brothers, Simon called Peter and his brother Andrew. They were casting a net into the lake, for they were fishermen. "'Come, follow me,' Jesus said, 'I will make you fishers of men.'"[167] What a change in vocation! It was a new beginning, not understood in all of its ramifications, but full of vision, promise, and hope.

In similar manner, many encounter Christ and are called to the vision and adventure of bringing others into relationship and discipleship with the Savior. This call has the potential for much more than discipleship. For many it may become a life commitment to vocational ministry. But before that can happen, there is much else that needs to occur. Let's follow the story.

THE COMMITMENT

The disciples followed Jesus very much as observers of his ministry throughout Galilee. They were watching and witnessing the healing of lepers, the paralysed, the lame, and the man with the withered hand. They saw the love and compassion of Jesus. They heard his teaching of the multitudes by Galilee. They saw his prayer vigils in the night wherein Jesus went up into a mountain to seek his Father's face They listened, enraptured by his Sermon on the Mount and his challenges to righteous living. They saw him raise the dead and respond to the challenges of the Pharisees. They saw him define his calling in relationship to his family. They listened, wondering about the meaning of many of his parables. In amazement, they saw him still the waters of the sea, calming

---

167 See: John 1:35-42; Mark 1:16-20; Matthew 4:15-22; Luke 5:1-11

their fears and anxiety. They experienced special and preparatory training around the area of Galilee.

Then the time for commitment came; Jesus declared emphatically, "The work of God is this: to believe in the one he has sent...I am the bread of life...All that the Father gives me will come to me, and whoever comes to me I will never drive away...I am the living bread that came down from heaven."[168] In response to these sayings, John tells us, "On hearing it, many of his disciples said, 'This is a hard teaching.'" Soon the disciples were grumbling amongst themselves and many left. Jesus asked the Twelve, "You do not want to leave too, do you?" This was the time of crisis, the time of decision, and Peter responded for them all, "Lord, to whom shall we go? You have the words of eternal life. We believe and know that you are the Holy One of God."[169] The die was cast. Jesus then assured them that he had chosen them.

A similar process happens in the lives of many of us who are called to ministry. It is the work of God, the ministry of the Spirit that leads to such clarification of our commitment. Others may encourage or help, but it is God and the work of the Spirit of God. This conviction matures in us a level of commitment, and at that moment we must respond. Either we turn back from full surrender or we to move forward into the uncertainty of what it means to be called and chosen of God for ministry. This is never an easy decision; if it seems easy, it has not been adequately weighed and the cost has not been anticipated with objectivity as to what ministry really is. But with clarification and commitment, one moves forward, perhaps with fear and trembling, but also with a sure knowledge of the faithfulness of the one whom we serve. The

---

168 John 6:25-59
169 John 6:60-71

call of Jesus to ministry and one's response of commitment will normally be preceded by an intimate following of him in one's life.

Challenges to commitment will come. Jesus was sharply attacked by the Pharisees and the Sadducees as they tested and rejected him. He used these occasions to warn the disciples of the *yeast* of these doubting, debating, and corrupting people.[170] Jesus challenged his followers about having eyes but not seeing the hand of God where it would have been evident to eyes of faith. When they proceeded on to Caesarea Philippi, Jesus tested the disciples. He asked, "Who do people say the Son of Man is? ... Who do you say I am?"[171] It is never enough to know what people say; God's call must be personalized. The one called and committed must clarify his personal conviction again and again, as it is repeatedly challenged by the opinions of others. Peter responds, "You are the Christ, the Son of the living God." It must be recognized that such assurance comes from the Father and is the foundation of all commitment to ministry. Commitment must be authenticated before the test of the life circumstances or the called one stands in jeopardy.

Challenge Met with Failure

Following this declaration of commitment, the disciples entered what must have been a tumultuous time for them. Much that happened was quite beyond their comprehension. Three were invited to witness the glorious experience of the Transfiguration. The opposition increased in intensity. Then,

---

170 Matthew 16:1-12; Mark 8:13-26
171 Mark 8:27-30; Matthew 16:13-30; Luke 9:18-21

Jesus began to speak more openly of his death. He rebuked the disciples for lack of faith and for turning children away from his blessing. Jesus became more forceful in addressing hypocrisy. He taught a concept of forgiveness that was beyond their imagination. He challenged their fleshly competition with one another for first place in his group. When the rich young ruler rejected Jesus, the disciples immediately began to wonder about their reward. They watched as Jesus was anointed for death. Then at the last Passover, Jesus declared that there was a traitor among them. Jesus addressed their fear and anxiety, but they had little understanding of what was about to happen. They were confused by many ambiguities that did not make sense to them.

Peter made a bold declaration: "Even if all fall away on account of you, I never will."[172] Jesus tells Peter tenderly that Satan desires to sift him as wheat is sifted. Not knowing the power of Satan, Peter replies, "Lord, I am ready to go with you to prison and to death."[173] His intention was laudable but he did not know the power of the foe.

The dark hour of Gethsemane demonstrated both the commitment of Jesus in facing the burden of man's sin on the cross and also the weakness of human commitment. The disciples were overcome with sleep, and Jesus was left to agonize alone. During the trial of Jesus, just as Jesus had foreseen, Peter denied him three times. Apart from John, all the others seem to have disappeared. All four Gospels record Peter's humiliation and sorrow, and we can readily empathize with him. Anyone who has faced the pressure of the crowd, the loss of support of peers or witnessed the humiliation of a loved one,

---

[172] Mark 14:29
[173] Luke 22:33

and sensed the abject inability to comprehend or forestall what was happening, will understand Peter's experience.

Many pastors with whom I have journeyed have experienced many of the emotions Peter must have experienced that night. It is usually not from denial of Christ, but from other painful experiences in ministry. These emotions may arise from our own sense of inadequacy or the insensitivity of others and their lack of responsiveness to our leadership. They may arise from not knowing how to deal with dysfunctional church communities, or rejection by fellow believers and peers. Many pastors walk this path of pain and despair in ministry when rejected by churches or when unable to find a place of ministry. The pain accumulates and becomes overwhelming. It is heartbreaking to watch pastors experience these things (as shared earlier in this book) and so many of them drop out of ministry in despair. They can identify with Peter in his grief and even in knowing the Savior is risen, they find it easier to "go fishing" than to find healing for their pain of rejection or loss in ministry. There must be a more effective response to those overwhelmed by the grief of loss or the pain of rejection and self-condemnation that parallels the experience of Peter so closely.

Restoration and Recommissioning

Witnessing the crucifixion was sheer agony for the followers of Jesus. Nevertheless, when word came that Jesus was alive, Peter and John rushed immediately to the tomb. Still reeling from the trauma of Jesus's horrific death and not knowing that the Scriptures foretold the resurrection, they continued bewildered until Jesus showed himself to Peter and the others. Even after the many appearances of Jesus to his disciples,

Chapter 10: A Biblical Account of Commitment, Failure, and Restoration

Peter decided to go fishing in the Sea of Tiberias.[174] However, Jesus knew where to find them.

One cannot exaggerate the significance of Jesus meeting with his disciples once again at the sea of Tiberias.[175] With typical enthusiasm in seeing Jesus, Peter leaped into the sea and headed for shore in response to Jesus` question, "Friends haven't you any fish?" After that memorable breakfast, Jesus spoke to Peter alone. He clarified Peter's love. Earlier when Jesus had told Peter of his temptation and denial, he said, "I have prayed for you, Simon, that your faith may not fail. And when you have turned back, strengthen your brothers."[176] Peter's restoration was a fulfillment of the prayer of Jesus. One might explore the relationship between faith and denial. The prayer of Jesus was that Peter's faith not fail. Perhaps, denial does not express a loss of faith as much as a lapse of confidence in the moment of confusion, loneliness, despair, and disillusionment. Denial may at times portray the effect of trauma.

The key question in this exchange is, "Simon son of John, do you truly love me more than these?" Peter's earlier triple denial is now replicated by his triple affirmation. These men were called to become fishers of men. On an earlier occasion as Peter was told of the denial he would soon be making, he was also told that when restored, he was to strengthen his brothers.[177] He is here told to feed and shepherd the flock of God. The clarification of his love for the Lord was the foundation upon which his future was to be built. Jesus does not focus on the past; Peter's denial is irrelevant at this point. His

---

174 John 21:2-3
175 See John 21
176 Luke 22:31-32
177 Luke 22:32

present state of love is the issue, for only that love will sustain him in the ministry that lies before him.

So it is with those passing through the experience of transition. Transition may end one ministry but when the grief (or healing that is required) is complete, we are to affirm our love for the Lord and enter into a renewed commitment to ministry. We must not let the trauma of transition turn us aside from our foundational commitment to the Lord and our call to serve him with our lives. To those called of God, the other side of transition is further ministry even if the location or nature of the ministry is different.

The important reality here is that Jesus restored Peter to the role for which he had called him: "Feed my sheep." And Jesus urged him to continue to do so until he was old and incapable of caring for himself. The call to a vocation of serving Christ has no retirement clause. "Follow me" is a life project that must not be distracted by the ministry given to others. Vocation is not something to be survived until we achieve retirement. Vocational ministry is to form the fulfillment of one's life and one's call to the end. That is what Peter was commissioned to do.

What Jesus wants for John is no business of Peter's. The responsibility of each of us is to attend to our own calling and to find peace with that in the context of our love for the Lord. We must move beyond the disciple's distraction as they followed Jesus – that being, their competition with one another. No human faculty can reach the height of knowing Jesus or the Father fully. However, our love will access the heart of God for our sustenance in ministry. The focus must be singular. Peter's restoration to ministry is a precious and important record of God's intention for each of us.

We too may have experienced the confusion, despair, anxiety, and exhaustion that the disciples experienced in the week before Christ's death. We may have experienced failure, or felt that we have failed because of personal dysfunction, or because of the cruelty and temptation of Satan. However, once called, we have an advocate with the Father who intercedes for us, to stay the hand of Satan. He will also restore us to our calling. We may need to learn how to cope with much that is mysterious and beyond our comprehension in the workings of God. Jesus wishes to fulfill his calling in us just as he did in Peter. Restoration and renewal are in the heart of God for everyone who has been called to serve him.

This is an important message for all who are engaged in ministry. The trials of ministry are illustrated in the lives of Moses, Nehemiah, Gideon, David, Paul, and many others in the Scriptures. Whether one's experience in ministry has been happy or difficult, the transition from one ministry to another involves a predictable pattern of change. It is the part of wisdom to seek understanding of the processes that accompany change in ministry; transitions in ministry can become a time of renewal and transformation. Achieving some objectivity through a reflective pause may produce valuable understanding and learning about oneself and the faithfulness of God. A productive and rewarding refining of our understanding of God's gifting of us for ministry can occur. It can lead to renewed commitment and recommissioning through the guidance of his Spirit. I invite you to explore your experience of transition.

> The Lord will guide you always;
> He will satisfy your needs in a sun-scorched land
> and will strengthen your frame. You will be like a
>   well-watered garden,
> like a spring whose waters never fail.
>
> Isaiah 58:11

QUESTIONS FOR REFLECTION:

Was my transition brought about by my actions, or those of others? If at my initiation, was it a redefinition or refinement of the ministry I am most clearly called to enter into? If initiated by others, what must I do to free myself from any residual issues that need to be addressed before I move on? Would the help of someone else bring me more objectivity toward exploring and understanding my transition experience? It will be helpful to write responses to these questions and explore one's experience. Writing things down will bring some degree of objectivity.

Chapter 11

Postscript: Where Do We Go from Here?

> And now the Sovereign Lord has sent me, with his Spirit.
> This is what the Lord says—your Redeemer, the Holy One of Israel:
> "I am the Lord your God who teaches you what is best for you,
> Who directs you in the way you should go."
>
> Isaiah 48:16-17

Perhaps you have been able to see snatches of your own experience in what has been shared in these pages. They have presented a composite picture of bits and pieces from the experiences of many. Many of the suggestions given here could be further developed and expanded; they have been briefly presented to limit the size of the book. They may be considered pointers that you could expand and elaborate. Let me invite you to become a participant with others in ministry as they journey through the turbulence of transition. Looking at the experience sequentially in stages is usually helpful.

The achievement of understanding the experience is the first step. Only with understanding through the wisdom that

God provides can our eyes of faith be opened to explore the learning inherent in the opportunities presented by transition. God is sovereign but we have to have the eyes to see through the shadows of experience to observe his hand at work. We begin with faith and endure with hope that in each experience he is at work to conform us to the image of Christ.

We do not have to present answers to others but we are called to come alongside them to bear burdens and offer them the comfort with which God has comforted us. We can do this for each other. Many have stood with me when I was in need of a fellow traveller through the hard places. The greatest resource along with the Spirit of God is others who express acceptance of us fully and in so doing encourage us to become all we can be, by God's grace. One possibility is to interact with fellow-pastors around the questions that are at the end of each chapter. Exploring the promises that are within the passages at the beginning and end of each chapter will expand our awareness of the commitments and promises God made to those who seek to follow him. His faithfulness is assured.

You would benefit me by sharing your story or your questions or criticisms of the perspectives I have tried to articulate in this book. Together, we might more fully understand the experience of transition. You may wish to contact me through the web site related to this book. My prayer for you is that God will fulfill his purposes in your life of ministry and that you celebrate joy in serving him.

Questions for Reflection

What are the evidences of the hand of God in my experience? How do I rate my confidence and faith in his sovereign leading on a scale of one to ten? Have I cared for the interests of my spouse and family as well as I could? Could I clarify any issues for them to help them in understanding? What fellow-pastor do I know who would benefit from my acceptance and affirmation?

> You are my servant, Israel, in whom I will display my splendor ...
> And now the Lord says—he who formed me in the womb to be his servant ...
> for I am honoured in the eyes of the Lord
> and my God has been my strength.
>
> Isaiah 49:3-5

About the Author

It has been helpful to me to have summary information about authors I read; it provides a context into which I can place what they are discussing. Since this summary covers almost eight decades, it will hit only the highlights that provide a context for this book.

My faith journey began as a teenager. My excitement in hearing the Gospel for the first time started me on a great adventure in faith and life. Being the first in my family of six siblings to have the opportunity to go to secondary school, I struggled between despair and excitement. My motivation for going to Seminary was to acquire biblical knowledge so as to teach a class of nine-year-old boys. While attending a Baptist Seminary for a Bachelor's degree in theology, I engaged in pioneering churches. Over a period of seven years we started three churches. Two frustrations developed: I felt ill equipped to disciple individuals or to deal with church tensions. Further education seemed the best answer. This was made possible by working in Correctional services while completing graduate degrees in psychology and theology.

My next transition was into Bible College and Seminary teaching and counselling of students. The last three years of this twelve-year period was as Assistant to the President. For almost eight years following that I served as General Director of a large inner-city ministry, Yonge Street Mission, in Toronto. Eighteen years as Director of Counselling Services at Missionary Health Institute and International Health Management brought me to retirement in 2005.

During the years since 1970, I also served as president of our Baptist denomination, served an international mission board (African Inland Mission), provided psychological assessments, orientation programs and debriefing for several thousand missionaries (from over twenty-five different mission organizations), and visited over twenty countries to respond in consulting and conflict issues among missionaries and nationals. Many on-field training seminars for missionary leaders and nationals were conducted. Providing counselling, consultation and conflict resolution for churches and pastors during these years was a major involvement. My wife and I provided a retreat centre for missionaries, their children and pastoral families for eleven years. During that time over 1,600 people came to our home for one to fourteen days for retreat and counselling.

A major influence on me was the opportunity to be involved with seven other professionals who provided research for a dozen mission organizations to study the issues surrounding the boarding experience of children, transition experiences for families and the contributors to family success in missions. In retirement, I continue to consult with churches of different denominations and to walk with pastors through difficulties and through the turbulence of transition.

glennctaylor35@gmail.com